FIAT LUX

THE UNIVERSITY OF CALIFORNIA

FIAT LUX

ANSEL ADAMS

NANCY NEWHALL

THE UNIVERSITY OF CALIFORNIA

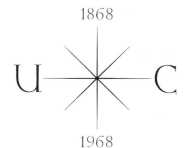

1868

1968

A CENTENNIAL PUBLICATION OF THE UNIVERSITY OF CALIFORNIA

McGRAW-HILL BOOK COMPANY
NEW YORK TORONTO LONDON SYDNEY

Charter Day, 1964, Hearst Greek Theatre, Berkeley

FIAT LUX: THE UNIVERSITY OF CALIFORNIA

DEDICATED TO THOSE WHO WILL MAKE THE FUTURE

The Pleiades. Photograph by Lick Observatory, University of California

INTRODUCTION

To look at the University of California is to look at California itself—its land, its people, and their problems—into the civilization rushing toward us from the future. There are few aspects of California, or of this civilization, whose first shapes are already sharply visible against still nebulous but galactic potentials, with which the University is not concerned.

When Clark Kerr, then president of the University, asked us to undertake this survey in words and photographs for the University's centennial, he challenged us to project, as far as possible, "the next hundred years." Literally impossible, of course, because you cannot—as yet!—photograph a thought beginning to stir in the minds of a hundred, or a thousand, or a million different men, nor will any responsible scholar allow premature publication of his ideas and theories.

Nevertheless, we took Kerr's challenge as our general directive. Conceivably, there have been or will be more arduous periods in which to photograph the University; this period was difficult enough. On many campuses, the University was being torn down, rebuilt and expanded at a rate unbelievable, perhaps, except by eyewitnesses. Buildings were being demolished and carted away. Bulldozers were excavating new sites and roads, and carving out new landscapes. Cranes were lifting up girders and swinging shapes of precast concrete into place. Saplings were being staked up, and new plantings soaked by sprinklers. In 1964, when we made our first panoramic tour, there was nothing at Irvine but a few skeletal piers, nothing at San Diego but a building and a half, while at Santa Cruz the Chancellor had set up office in an old cookhouse. Visually, the University was in metamorphosis.

Internally, perhaps, there has never been a more illuminating period through which to view the University. The excitement of seeing so many plans, hopes and ideas materializing simultaneously embraced not only the University, from Regents to freshmen, but also the surrounding communities.

In the course of creating this comprehensive survey of the total University and its effect on the people and the land of California, we made many visits to each of the nine campuses and the major scientific and agricultural experiment stations. We wish it were possible to thank individually the hundreds of people who have helped in our search for understanding and the often elusive essential image—the chancellors and information officers of each campus, the deans of the many schools and colleges and of extension, the directors of the great scientific laboratories, the farm advisors of several counties, the professors and students who patiently endured the insistent camera eye and answered innumerable questions.

To penetrate to the central concept expressive of a place or a project was often exceedingly difficult, and finally achieved only after several trials. Neither the contrived, exotic situation nor the careless "candid" snapshot are compatible with a truthful statement. Most laboratories, no matter how world-shaking their achievements, contain much the same hardware or glassware; classrooms, with a few exceptions, are alike everywhere; conferences and colloquia resemble each other interchangeably. One quickly runs out of visual variety. Yet there is no limit to the depth of human qualities of both faculty and students; the interactions and events are, to each individual, unique and very important. Our problem was to create some semblance of the total effect, the symbol rather than the enumeration.

During the last three years, thousands of subjects were encountered and studied, many hundreds photographed, reams of text written and rewritten. Many sequences and combinations of text and photographs were considered, and rejected as too detailed or too long. A favored photograph or passage of text would often be given up in deference to a more explicit image-and-word statement.

It is not possible to compress the University of California into 192 pages—to depict all aspects of student life, or to record all the popular buildings and vistas! Everyone who has been concerned in the making of this book will regret the inevitable omissions—and none more than the authors. So when you look upon a certain professor or student and wonder, perhaps, why x was chosen instead of y, remember that x, in this book, represents y and perhaps a thousand more, all equally deserving of representation in these pages.

The entire photographic archive will be deposited in the Bancroft Library at Berkeley, where it will serve not only as a record of the University at this period but as a source for future publications and other uses by the University. The present selection represents, to the best intentions and abilities of the authors, a brief outline of what we have seen and understood of the scope, grandeur and quality of the University of California.

To list all those to whom we are indebted would require something on the scope of the University directory; our profound gratitude to you all. To those most intimately and enduringly concerned, our appreciation goes first to Verne A. Stadtman, Centennial Editor, and his patient and efficient staff, who have checked facts, illuminated approaches, typed and retyped text, and forwarded it, with celerity, to the authorities concerned, for comment and correction; to Liliane De Cock, for staunch and steadfast assistance in every phase of this project, including the making of three dummies; to Charles R. Wood and his associates for their meticulous care with the printing; and to Adrian Wilson, typographer and printer, whose skill and perception have helped immeasurably in the design and production of this book.

ANSEL ADAMS
NANCY NEWHALL

Multidimensional Model Illustrating Population Dynamics,
Hastings Natural History Reservation

CONTENTS

I THE CHALLENGE

In 1849, the year of the Gold Rush, thousands of people were converging on the huge, wild, still scarcely mapped territory of California. Many died on the way, in the mountains and the deserts, in the swamps of the Isthmus, and in the storms and shipwrecks of the long sea voyage around Cape Horn. Nevertheless, the population was growing by leaps and bounds; in spite of its remoteness, half a continent away from the rest of the nation, California would soon be a state. It was in chaos and confusion. The Constitutional Convention, meeting in Monterey, declared: "We are without a dollar belonging to the people, nor can we raise one without levying taxes, which no population was ever in a worse condition to bear...the laborers have abandoned their ranches and gone to the mines. Hence the owners of property are nearly ruined..., the vast majority of people have no property to be taxed except the gold they dig out of the earth...."

Anticipating, even in the midst of such destitution, the founding of a state university, "with such branches as the public convenience may demand, for the promotion of literature, the arts and sciences," the Convention made provision to protect and improve such lands or funds as might "be granted or reserved by the United States or any person or persons" for its support. "If we have the means here," said one delegate with an optimism destined to become characteristic of California, "we can procure the necessary talent; we can bring the president of the Oxford University here by offering a sufficient salary." They petitioned Congress for public lands, but the two townships eventually granted did not yield sufficient funds.

Meanwhile a few private academies and colleges were established. In Oakland, a group of Congregationalists and Presbyterians, led by the Reverend Samuel H. Willey and the Reverend Henry Durant, founded the Contra Costa Academy, which opened in 1853 in a rented *fandango* house. Two years later it was incorporated as the College of California; it had buildings and a campus of sorts, but its trustees began hunting for a larger, permanent site more in keeping with its aspirations for the future. Eventually they decided on a hillside, some miles north of Oakland, which looked down on the glittering Bay of San Francisco, across to the city on its many hills, and out through the Golden Gate to the Pacific. Here, one day in 1866, on an outcropping of rock at the base of steep hills, they were watching two ships stand out toward the Golden Gate when one of them quoted the famous lines by the philosopher, Berkeley:

> "Westward the course of empire takes its way;
> The four first acts already past.
> A fifth shall close the drama with the day;
> Time's noblest offspring is the last."

The proposal was made that they should call the site *Berkeley*.

Fund-raising was difficult, due to the instabilities and anxieties of the times, first the Vigilantes in San Francisco and then the Civil War and its aftermath throughout the nation. Willey went East on fund-raising tours; Durant went begging to the new tycoons across the bay, and sometimes despaired. "Individuality is carried to an extreme in California...idealism seems lost from the mass of the people. They are sensualists and materialists...."

In 1862, Abraham Lincoln signed the Morrill Land Grant Act, which offered public lands to any state which would found "a college of agriculture and the mechanical arts." California's share would be 150,000 acres. The legislature in 1866 voted to establish a College of Agriculture, Mining and the Mechanical Arts. The College of California then made a remarkable offer: to transfer its buildings and lands to the state on condition that a new institution, "a complete university," be established, in which the arts and sciences should be taught as well as agriculture, mining and engineering. The legislature accepted. The Organic Act creating the University of California was signed by the governor on March 23, 1868, a date celebrated ever since as Charter Day.

The motto chosen for the new University was:
Let There Be Light—FIAT LUX.

"First it is a university, and not a high school, or a college, nor an academy of sciences, nor an industrial school which we are charged to build. Some of these features may indeed be included...but the university means more than any or all of them. The university is the most comprehensive term which can be employed to indicate a foundation for the promotion and diffusion of knowledge—a group of agencies organized to advance the arts and sciences of every sort, and train young men as scholars for all the intellectual callings of life....

"It is not the University of Berlin, nor of New Haven, which we are to copy...it is the University of this State. It must be adapted to this people, to their public and private schools, to their peculiar geographical position, to the requirements of their new society and their undeveloped resources....

"Science is the mother of California. Give us more and not less science; encourage the most thorough and prolonged search for the truth which is to be found in the rocks, the sea, the soil and air, the sun and the stars; in light and heat and magnetic forces; in plants and animals, and in the human frame; but let us also learn the lessons which are embodied in language and literature, in laws and institutions, in doctrines and opinions, in historical progress...."

> DANIEL COIT GILMAN
> Second President of the University, 1872–1875
> Inaugural Address

In the fall of 1869, the little University opened, still in Oakland, with forty students and a faculty of ten. Three months later its Regents abolished tuition. Thenceforth every qualified student who was a resident of California could enter the University free —an opportunity that, beyond question, contributed to the phenomenal growth of both California and its University. The quality of the education may be judged by the members of its first four-year graduating class, 1873, soon known as "the Twelve Apostles," who were to include a governor of the state, a mayor of Alameda, an engineer, a professor of mathematics, two lawyers, and a bank president; three of them were to serve as Regents.

The first years were turbulent. The income from the land grant funds and other endowments was insufficient; biennially the Regents had to appeal to the legislature for funds. Then a strong agricultural bloc, which had no use for the classical college or the notion that pure science had an important role to play in the future, and wanted immediate, practical results, raised a storm of criticism that threatened to abolish the Board of Regents and extinguish the University except for the Colleges of Agriculture, Mining, and Mechanic Arts. They also charged mismanagement of the land grant funds. The legislature, investigating, returned a clean ledger. The Regents, an able and powerful group of leading citizens, regained control. But dissension over the University's purpose and criticism of its administration lingered. In 1876, the legislature, after passionate debate and by a very narrow margin, defeated a move to detach the College of Agriculture from the University. Further attempts to alter the organic structure of the University by statute were ended in 1879 when a new state constitution, approved by the people of California, declared the University "a public trust... it shall be entirely independent of all political or sectarian influences, and kept free therefrom in the appointment of its regents and the administration of its affairs."

In spite of recurring storms, the University grew, decade by decade, college after college and station after station. In the 1870's, on the initiative of private donors, the University acquired a college of medicine and another of law in San Francisco, and the first United States Agricultural Experiment Station and a college of agriculture that would soon have few peers in the world were developed in Berkeley. In the 1880's the University's first great scientific station, Lick Observatory, was built. In the 1890's the college of mines attracted some of the University's first foreign students, and the University began reaching people throughout the state through Agricultural Extension and the University Extension. Toward the end of the 19th century, a halcyon period set in, an era of constructive competition with the new Stanford University at Palo Alto, and of splendid donations, including sponsorship of a comprehensive architectural design for the Berkeley campus. In the

1900's, came the University Farm at Davis, the Citrus Experiment Station at Riverside, and at La Jolla the beginning of the University's second great station, now known as the Scripps Institution of Oceanography. In 1910, Abraham Flexner, in his report on American education, listed the University of California as one of the leading universities in the country.

After World War I, and its aftermath, which shook the universities like the rest of the world, growth continued again. A "southern branch" of the University was established in Los Angeles. At Berkeley the already famous College of Engineering was being consulted on the planning and testing of such huge structures as the Golden Gate and Bay Bridges, and the Hoover and Shasta Dams. The invention of the cyclotron by Ernest O. Lawrence, a young physics professor at Berkeley, opened the Atomic Age and its world-shaking discoveries in high energy nuclear physics, chemistry, medicine, biology, industry, and warfare. Lawrence became the first of thirteen University faculty members who have won the Nobel Prize. In 1934, Berkeley was rated second in distinction only to Harvard. During World War II, some of its most brilliant and creative scientists and engineers were drafted into the vast, secret Manhattan Project, the most crucial of whose objectives was solving, before the Nazis did, the

problems of the atom bomb. In 1943 the United States asked the University of California to administer the first nuclear weapons plant; the site chosen was Los Alamos, New Mexico.

After World War II, population in California boomed as never before. The thousands of workers in the aircraft and shipyard industries, the thousands of servicemen stationed here briefly on their way to the Pacific, could not forget what they had glimpsed of life in California. They returned with their families to settle here. Veterans coming to finish their education under the G. I. Bill of Rights and high school students, whose numbers were growing almost geometrically, deluged the campuses. Along with the population explosion came the knowledge explosion: science was growing exponentially and so was industry. More people needed more knowledge than ever before. To University administrators it seemed as if a whole generation at once was clamoring at the gates for higher education.

The University, even in the middle of World War II, had begun planning to meet these problems. In 1944 President Robert Gordon Sproul called an All-University Faculty conference at Davis, where delegates talked for three days of the discoveries and developments made during the intensive research projects of wartime—many of course were still secret and could not be discussed—and what they would entail for the University when the tide of veterans came back again. Specialized laboratories, new classrooms and auditoriums, new research institutes —it took time to plan, fund and build such facilities. War surplus barracks could temporarily serve such purposes, but even permanent construction programs on the existing campuses would prove to be only stopgaps. What was needed was not only new campuses, but entire new faculties and new approaches to education in a rapidly changing society.

"We are just now perceiving that the University's invisible product, knowledge, may be the most powerful single element in our culture, affecting the rise and fall of professions, and even of social classes, of regions and even of nations....Knowledge is now central to society. It is wanted, even demanded, by more people and institutions than ever before.... Knowledge, today, is for everybody's sake."

CLARK KERR
President of the University, 1958–1967
from *The Uses of the University*, 1963

*Old Medical Building, now
demolished, San Francisco*

Small liberal arts colleges of the highest quality were developed at Santa Barbara College, a part of the University since 1944, and at Davis and Riverside. But the combined pressures of the population and knowledge explosions continued to mount; enrollment outran the wildest predictions. In 1958, anticipating an enrollment in excess of 118,000—an underestimate which has been revised upward—the University embarked on a program of expansion unprecedented in the history of education, to double its size and at the same time maintain its high academic reputation.

On the older campuses, such as Berkeley, San Francisco, and Los Angeles, which were enclosed by their cities, old buildings were demolished so that new and much larger facilities could be erected in their stead. Davis, Riverside and Santa Barbara became full general campuses. Sites for three new campuses were found—a large ranch at Santa Cruz, another at Irvine, and a long mesa above the Scripps Institution of Oceanography at La Jolla. For each campus the University recruited a faculty brilliant in both teaching and research, and encouraged them to initiate fresh and creative directions in education, to devise an academic plan that would differ in emphasis from the other campuses, and to seek ways to enrich the life as well as the learning of the individual undergraduate. Smaller classes, bringing student and teacher closer together, smaller residence halls centering on patios and fountains, academic buildings grouped around plazas and connected by terraces, colonnades, and tree-shaded paths—on these most campuses agreed, and leading architects and planners were called in to give these ideas form and space. Financed by state bond issues, generous private donations, and grants from foundations and the federal government, construction began on every campus.

In 1966, Clark Kerr, President of the University, could report that the number of general campuses had risen from two to eight, enrollment from 43,000 to 88,000, faculty from 4,000 to 7,000, Nobel Laureates from five to twelve. Nineteen new colleges and professional schools had been created, and sixty-one new institutes, centers and laboratories for organized research. In eight years the University had doubled both in size and distinction.

California itself, in the 1950's, was facing the problems of sudden and enormous growth. Thousands were coming into the state daily; an average fifteen hundred a day stayed. Cities began to sprawl out through suburb after suburb and merge with the next city. Urbanization was gouging the massive hills, bulldozing the orchards, and filling some of the world's richest agricultural valleys with ill-planned commercial housing. Traffic, snarling the highways, became, during rush hours, unmanageable; freeways began slicing through canyons and along the shores. New industries multiplied. Smog from the automobiles and the industries not only choked the cities, darkening the light and obscuring the distances, but, drifting through the mountain passes, killed crops in the inland valleys and damaged even the alpine forests. The need to escape from confusion and pollution and find pure air and clean water, space, quiet and wild beauty, was causing the destruction of these very qualities in the State and National Parks. The need for lumber was devastating whole watersheds, while the need for water increased with every new home, new city, new field irrigated.

In 1963 California became the most populous state in the nation. It faced the crisis of growth that earlier had slowly overwhelmed regions in the Eastern states and Europe, and would sooner or later confront every industrialized society on earth.

It stood to lose what it most loved and treasured—its magnificent landscape and brilliant climate, its easy, spacious, lavish way of living, its cosmopolitan cities—the whole proud young California civilization it had, during the last century, with the help of its University, evolved.

Never had it needed its University more. What happens—or does not happen—to California in its attempts to solve the problems of population and industrialization will affect the world.

The challenge to the University of California today is nothing less than to help bring forth the civilization of the future.

Freeways, Los Angeles

"Megalopolis: this phenomenon we have created has become one of the major problems of our times; a gargantuan monster, growing without apparent pattern or reason, which in many ways has brutalized the society. I speak not specifically of Los Angeles, but of nearly every community in the world.

"Megalopolis has created a whole range of complex problems which converge for solution on our universities. It is there that scholars apply their knowledge and imagination to the problems of urban design, air pollution, conservation of vital resources such as water, highway safety for a nation on wheels, and the massive human dilemmas stemming from the persistent failure of society to provide truly equal opportunity.

"It is no accident that universities are being called upon to solve these problems. The modern American university developed as a servant and friend of society."

FRANKLIN D. MURPHY
Chancellor at Los Angeles

II CITIES OF INTELLECT

Berkeley

Today, standing at the foot of the slope and looking up through park-like vistas at the buildings crowding this oldest and largest of the University's campuses, and on, past the soaring Campanile, up to the steep hills crowned by laboratories whose discoveries continue to influence the history of mankind—even an easterner, skeptical of western bombast, even a European, skeptical of American culture *in toto*, feels the indisputable presence of greatness. It is not the greatness of age—Berkeley is young as universities go —nor is it merely the nobility of the site nor the moments of architectural splendor. The greatness of Berkeley is that of the young genius who has begun to discover and apply his powers.

This sense of purpose and unfolding, increasing powers pervades the entire campus and its hurrying crowds of students and faculty. Berkeley is now at peak enrollment: 27,500 students, some 16,000 undergraduate, some 11,000 graduate. More than 2,500 of them come from nearly 100 different nations. Indian girls in saris, Africans in correct British dress, Orientals wearing Occidental clothes of exquisite line and color contribute a cosmopolitan brilliance to the multitude of casually dressed young Americans. Frequently, sermonizers holding forth from beyond the curb on Telegraph Avenue attract little knots of spectators. Much the same happens at the tables set up near Sather Gate, which has long served as Berkeley's Hyde Park. But the vast majority of students hurry past. There is so much to do at Berkeley—the 3,000 courses in seventy-two departments of instruction offered by fifteen colleges and schools, the cultural calendar crowded with music, dance, theater, exhibitions, and lectures by world-famous figures in every sphere of thought and action. Four years are not enough to encompass and absorb the riches of Berkeley. Most of this student body will not be content with the simple A.B. or B.S. degree. They will graduate

into the professional schools or into one of the fifty-eight great citadels of research to assist in the creation of new knowledge. And they will return at intervals throughout their lives for the renewal of learning.

Center and source of the University's far-flung system—the nine campuses (and more are needed) and the more than one hundred scientific and agricultural experiment stations which crisscross the state, Berkeley, in the opinion of the American Council of Education, is "the best-balanced, distinguished university in the country."

Corner of Sproul Plaza and Telegraph Avenue, Berkeley

"Each one of these is a personality searching for light in his own way. . . . Their concern with problems is genuine, and I find them far more knowledgeable than the students of my day. I find them engaged in more good causes than the students of my day. And I am sure that after going through much travail they will find answers to some problems that we have been unwilling to face."

EARL WARREN, Class of 1912
Chief Justice of the United States
Convocation, Berkeley, 1967

Class Change, Berkeley

"The University is not engaged in making ideas safe for students. It is engaged in making students safe for ideas."

CLARK KERR, 1961

Charter Day, Berkeley, 1964. Faculty and guests rise to greet
Adlai E. Stevenson, late Ambassador to the United Nations.

The faculty at Berkeley is one of the most eminent in the world. It includes ten living Nobel Laureates: Melvin Calvin, Owen Chamberlain, William F. Giauque, Donald A. Glaser, Edwin M. McMillan, John H. Northrop, Glenn A. Seaborg, Emilio Segrè, Wendell M. Stanley and Charles H. Townes. It holds first place among American universities in the number of recipients of Guggenheim Fellowships, and is second only to Harvard in members and fellows of the National Academy of Sciences and the National Academy of Arts and Sciences. Quite a number serve on advisory committees to the President of the United States and on boards of national and international importance. Those with the longest lists of honors and achievements are often also the greatest teachers.

This august body governs itself through the Academic Senate, which was established by the Organic Act of 1868. It has broad powers over conditions of student admission, requirements for degrees, courses of instruction, advice on employment of academic personnel, and other matters.

During its first quarter-century, when presidents were coming and going and the Regents steered the little University through storm after storm, the Senate was weak. Perhaps its most creative act was its resolution, in 1870, that "Young Ladies be admitted into the University on equal terms, in every respect, with young men." Most of its time in those years appears to have been spent in coping with the high spirits of youth and other matters of student discipline. It was beginning to assert its authority when Benjamin Ide Wheeler, in 1899, became president. A distinguished scholar and an able administrator, Wheeler raised the University to true greatness. He sought out the best men to be had and brought them to Berkeley. Some of the leading scholars of their time, they were not men easily dominated even by Wheeler, who became increasingly dictatorial with age and illness. Many of them, like Wheeler himself, had spent their post-graduate years at various universities in Germany, then the world center of learning and especially science. World War I, with its anti-German hysteria, cost some University members their jobs, and even damaged the prestige of Wheeler. In 1918 the Regents gave many of his powers to a Council of Deans, who, in the face of grave economic problems precipitated by the war and post-war periods, tried to continue

his arbitrary policies without his skill. In 1919–1920 the faculty, many of whom now bore the highest medals of England, France, and the United States, rose in a firm, orderly revolt. They won, through negotiation with the Regents, a voice in determining the academic budget and the right to recommend appointments, promotions and dismissals of their colleagues. They also won more authority and autonomy for the Academic Senate and for members of the various departments to conduct their own affairs.

The second crisis was again post-war. During World War II, many of the faculty had been engaged in highly secret projects of crucial importance to the survival of the Free World. Their loyalty had been checked and rechecked constantly, as a routine security measure. Consequently they were in no mood to accept, in addition to the usual loyalty oath sworn by every state employee, a special anti-Communist oath requested by the Regents during another time of national hysteria that led many state and local governments to impose such oaths on college and university faculties. The faculty resented the implication that the intellectual, per se, is politically suspect. Some refused to sign, some resigned, others were dismissed. After many months of recriminations and a court suit, the Regents withdrew the oath and reimbursed and reinstated such faculty "non-signers" as would consent to return. It took some time to restore morale; nevertheless, an important principle had been reaffirmed: freedom of thought and expression are essential to the University's purpose, the pursuit of truth.

The academic reforms and innovations instigated by Sproul and accelerated by Kerr were proceeding on all campuses when the mass demonstrations of 1964 and 1965 broke out at Berkeley. The faculty responded to many underlying issues of unrest, and were particularly concerned for the undergraduates wearing IBM cards in protest against the impersonal, mechanized education they felt they were receiving. Investigation and evaluation of actual conditions and grievances have led the faculty to vigorous action and the exploration of new approaches, all leading to closer communication between faculty and undergraduates.

The University of California Marching Band

Formed in 1891 to perform during military drills and University ceremonies, the Marching Band soon found itself famous and performing at state events and ceremonies such as the San Francisco Mid-Winter Fair of 1894, the dedication of the State Capitol in 1908, the Panama-Pacific Exposition in 1915—which celebrated the opening of the Panama Canal—and the Golden Gate Exposition of 1939. Its travels abroad have included such events as the 1958 Brussels World's Fair. Currently composed of 120 members, with twenty reserves, it is the only university band in the country to have its own residence hall, a gift of its alumni.

Berkeley now has 165,000 living alumni, and they have quite literally gone forth across the world. Some measure of their energy and excellence was given by President John F. Kennedy, in 1962: "When I observe the men who surround me in Washington—when I reflect that the Secretary of State, the Secretary of Defense, the Chairman of the Atomic Energy Commission, the Director of the Central Intelligence Agency, and the Ambassador to India are all graduates or former students of this University—I am forced to confront an uncomfortable truth, and so are you: that the New Frontier may well owe more to Berkeley than to Harvard." As alumni, they have made many important contributions to the University, raising funds for such buildings as the new Student Union and other campus improvements. They have provided thousands of undergraduate and special opportunity scholarships.

California Memorial Stadium

A gift of the alumni commemorating the University students who gave their lives in World War I, the great stadium, designed by John Galen Howard, holds 77,000 people. On Charter Day, 1962, when President John Fitzgerald Kennedy spoke, seats on the field swelled the audience to a record 92,000. The main athletic event of the year is, of course, the Big Game between the Bears and the Stanford Indians. Some of the old "CAL" spirit then stirs the vast and diverse campus. Balloons are loosed from the

Campanile. President Emeritus Sproul leads the parade, with its bands, floats, skits, and antics of Oski, the clown bear mascot.

The game itself is celebrated for its rival card stunts, such as the huge CAL which ripples across the rooter section as if written by a giant pen. Afterwards, whether the axe, that ancient trophy of victory, has gone back to Stanford or not, alumni, rooters, and guests of both universities swarm to the field to greet old friends.

San Francisco

Hugh H. Toland, a young physician trained at the University of Transylvania, who had studied under various European physicians, caught the Gold Rush fever and came to California to find, as usual, little gold, but quite a flourishing practice. And two remedies he called "anti-syph" and "anti-scroph," sold by mail order over the state, brought him something of a fortune.

The Mission Center of San Francisco in 1850 had 850 inhabitants; by 1860, 40,000. Schools, colleges, and universities were springing up, and folding. Toland decided to found a college of medicine, and acquired a faculty of ten, mostly from the recently disbanded medical school of the University of the Pacific. In 1864, in a high-arched Victorian building on Stockton Street, conveniently near the County Hospital and Home for Inebriates, the college opened its doors to eight students. Toland appears to have had high standards of excellence in teaching, but his school was torn by dissension almost from the start. By 1870 he had lost most of his faculty to a rival school and had only one student, who, it has been suggested, was too weak to walk out. At this low point, Toland went to his bitter enemy, Dr. Richard Beverly Cole, a leading practitioner and political figure—"King Cole of California"—who had actually accused Toland of malpractice resulting in the death of James King, editor of a local newspaper, who had been shot by a county supervisor. Perhaps it is a measure of both men that they got together, Toland appointing Cole as dean of his school, and Cole thenceforth fighting for the little college. It was Cole who concluded the negotiations with Daniel Coit Gilman, then briefly president of the University of California, through which the Toland College became, in 1873, the medical branch of the young University. That same year, the college absorbed a college of pharmacy, and then, in 1881, established a school of dentistry. It was Cole, again, who, when Mayor Adolph Sutro was outlining his visions for the heights out toward Land's End, persuaded him to donate land at the foot of what is now Sutro's Forest as the site for the new buildings needed by the now rapidly expanding medical college. There were objections to the remoteness of this new site, so far from the center of town; it was this same remoteness that saved the three new

buildings of the Affiliated Colleges from the fire following the 1906 earthquake. Several hospitals downtown were destroyed; to help the thousands of injured, the University set up a treatment center as a public service. Its value was immediately apparent, and the function of the medical school in the life of the community perceived to be essential. From the two floors in the medical school building which were then converted into a hospital, the University's involvement with community service has steadily expanded, through its hospitals and clinics, its research institutes, its centers for specialized care, and its programs for continuing education, both professional and lay, in the health sciences.

San Francisco Medical Center, from Golden Gate Park; California Academy of Sciences in the foreground

Among the center's many distinguished contributions are those of the George Williams Hooper Foundation, its oldest research group, founded in 1896, which discovered the sterilization methods on which the modern canning industry is based and also the control of certain animal-borne diseases, such as plague. Its Department of Radiology achieved the first motion pictures of the heart *in vivo* (1920's) and, in close collaboration with the Lawrences, the early use of million volt x-rays, the first use of radioisotopes in human patients, and the first treatment with cyclotron-produced fast neutrons. The Cardiovascular Research Institute has discovered how to manage asphyxia of the newborn, estimated to kill 25,000 babies a year in the United States alone. These are only a few; new research groups add continually to the list.

Tall towers have now replaced the old buildings of the Affiliated Colleges. A city within a city, the center looks down from its magnificent hillside site over San Francisco to the Golden Gate, the bay, and the Pacific. Dreams of expanding it into a general campus of the University, as Davis and Riverside grew from their experiment station cores, have not yet materialized; it is easy to visualize it as becoming a great university set like a crown to one of the great cities of the world. It prefers to continue to grow into its own vision of the future as a center for the study of the ecology of man.

Davis

Davis, once the University Farm, then the College of Agriculture, became in 1959 a full-scale campus of the University. The old silo stands beside the coffee shop; the octagonal pavilion originally built for the judging of livestock has been transformed into a Shakespearean theater with the apron in the pit; and there is a superb plow kept as an object of art in the court of the sculpture workshop. The flat, dull, hot plains have become a park; trees, planned and planted before construction began, now begin to shade courts and malls.

Davis now offers graduate degrees in more than 50 fields of study, and the number of undergraduate students enrolled in letters and science is about four times the number in agriculture. The campus expands continually: a School of Engineering keyed to aerospace projects; Schools of Law and Medicine; a new and powerful cyclotron; a laboratory for museology, where the problems of running museums and of restoring works of art are taught; and the nation's largest primate colony—ten thousand animals for biomedical research, through which discoveries that have saved millions of lives have already been made.

With all this expansion, Davis resists the frenetic pressures of urbanization. It was perhaps the first campus within the University wherein nearly everybody took to bicycles and shanks' mare, and many roads were closed to automobiles. It has not lost its open air vitality and hospitality: the annual Picnic Day, run by students for all comers, features a parade, fashion show, sheep dog trial, melodrama, and open house in all departments. On Labor Day—February 29th of each Leap Year—students and faculty throw all their energies into something that needs doing, such as demolishing an obsolete building, often accomplishing it before noon, and then have a vast barbeque and, in the evening, a dance.

Dramatic Art Building in Fine Arts complex, Davis

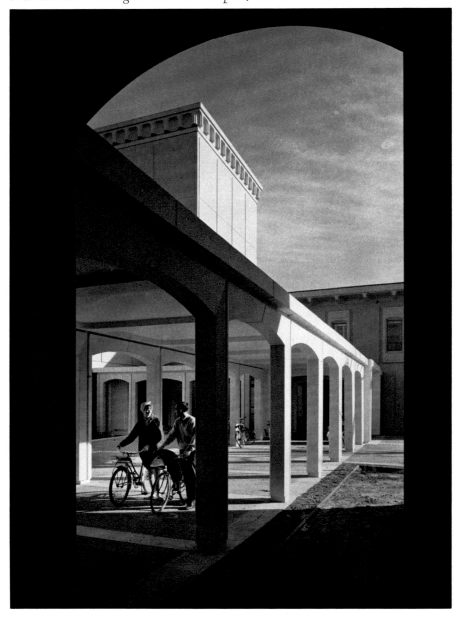

Class Change, Davis

"The ability and the willingness to take responsibility, to go to the lonely outposts of thought and action,
and to persuade others to follow you there—truly,
this ability is the rarest of commodities in the world
…we live in a world of tremendous numbers of
mass pressures, of enormous forces working for
the leveling out of talent and conformity of opinion.
The only way to keep this a good world, and to make
it better, is to assert creative and constructive
individualism, which to me is another way
of saying leadership."

EMIL M. MRAK
Chancellor at Davis

27

Genetics Field Trip

G. Ledyard Stebbins, professor of genetics, is a foremost authority on organic evolution. His passion for inquiring into its causes has led him recently into developmental and biochemical genetics. In *Plantago insularis,* a plantain found in hot deserts, which has four "beautiful" chromosomes and a life cycle of only six to eight weeks, he has found a plant species he believes may be as valuable to geneticists as the fly *Drosophila.* To test the hypothesis that evolution can be pressed forward and twenty million years of mutation compressed into perhaps twenty, he has crossed two strains of *Plantago* with the aim of causing their progeny to become adapted to a different climate. A man capable of encapsulating genetics in a nursery rhyme, Stebbins is a brilliant teacher, and his enthusiasm is contagious. Here he leads a group of graduate students to compare mutations in oats.

"Because of the shift the gene was changed—
  Because of the gene the protein was changed—
  Because of the protein the cell was changed—
  Because of the cell the blood was changed—
  Because of the blood the man was changed—
  Because of the man the kingdom was changed—
  And all for the shift of a hydrogen atom."

G. LEDYARD STEBBINS

School of Veterinary Medicine

From all over California and nearby states, people bring animals to the clinic at Davis, where their treatment is part of the clinical teaching program. A cow in need of an abdominal operation, a dog with a bad fracture, or a horse with a rare eye disease receives medical treatment in the most modern clinical facilities in the nation. The doctors and technicians use many of the same techniques developed for human medicine. Often the only difference is the species and size of the equipment in some of the operating rooms—there is one at Davis equipped especially for horses and cows.

Large Animal Clinic, Davis. Dr. John D. Wheat explains a diagnosis to graduate students

29

Los Angeles

Like the great medieval universities on the Continent, UCLA is urban—not only surrounded by the city, but intimately and deeply related to it. In 1915, the University, recognizing the sudden rise in population and, consequently, in the need for higher education in Southern California, opened in Los Angeles a headquarters for University Extension. These programs were so enthusiastically attended that the University, two years later, established an annual summer session. When, in 1919, Governor William D. Stephens signed the legislation transferring the grounds, buildings, and records of the old Los Angeles State Normal School to the University of California, it marked the culmination of years of effort by Regent Edward A. Dickson and other dedicated citizens to establish a "southern branch" of the University in Los Angeles. Within a few years it became obvious that the old campus on Vermont Avenue was too small for the rapidly growing young institution, and the Regents finally selected 383 acres of rolling hills at the foot of the Santa Monica Mountains, from which one could look across Los Angeles to the Pacific. The owners of the land offered to sell the site for one million dollars, and the neighboring cities of Los Angeles, Beverly Hills, Santa Monica, and Venice raised nearly the whole amount through bond issues.

The site suggested Italy—the rolling hills, the brilliant sunlight, the glimpses of the blue sea—and the first buildings, such as Royce Hall, named after the philosopher Josiah Royce, and the Library, were modeled after cathedrals and universities in Milan, Bologna, and Verona. Built of red brick, with cast stone trim and tiled roofs, their domes and towers and arched portals flank the original Quadrangle, from which the brick stairway and terra-cotta balustrades of the Janss Steps lead down to the playing fields. From this central theme the campus has developed along courts and malls interconnected by stairs. The hilltops have been leveled, and an arroyo filled in; concern for the noble use of urban open spaces, which characterizes great cities and great civilizations, continues to be the dynamic principle of planning on this campus.

Class Change, Royce Hall and the Quadrangle, UCLA

The North Campus: Sculpture Court, Social Sciences Building,
and Research Library from the Dickson Art Center, UCLA

If Los Angeles is concerned with its University, the University in turn is profoundly concerned with Los Angeles—with its tremendous problems as a sudden megalopolis and its equally tremendous potentials. The cultural awakening which has swept over what Aldous Huxley once called "the city of dreadful joy" is due in no small part to UCLA's meteoric rise to distinction.

Second in size and enrollment only to Berkeley among the University's campuses, UCLA now possesses a vast Medical Center, which includes a hospital caring for one hundred thousand patients a year and the internationally known Brain Research Institute; it has a new spiral ridge cyclotron, and is one of the chief national centers for the space sciences. More even than the sciences, UCLA emphasizes the arts and the humanities, and the understanding of other societies and civilizations through their art, music, dance, and theater. The new North Campus, one of whose entrances is through the Social Sciences building, is a proud symbol of the urban and international civilization Los Angeles envisions in the future: the Research Library, the new Dickson Art Center, and the Theater Arts building, including the superbly equipped Macgowan Theater, look down on a great plaza where crowds may flow through wide malls and and terraces and yet leave undisturbed the students sitting by the fountains or little patios around a sculpture.

Los Angeles believes urbanization is inevitable; the University's responsibility is to reach into every aspect of the onrushing twenty-first century, to face it without resentment or regret, and to solve its problems.

"Mankind in its current need and agony," Chancellor Franklin D. Murphy believes, is the University's chief concern, and its function is to provide "leadership for a world crying out for the solution to an ever-growing avalanche of real problems, needs and expectations....

"We must be in the library, but we must also be in Watts. We must be in the laboratory, but we must also be on the moon. We will be in the lecture rooms, but we will also be in the operating rooms. Without apology, indeed with undisturbed and I hope growing commitment, we will serve the world of pure scholarship and the world of man and his problems, and both with distinction.

"This we will do within the ancient University tradition of the free market place of ideas where all matters are open for discussion and analysis, without fear of retribution, and where dissent is as necessary as agreement for the vitality and integrity of the dialogue."

Sculpture by Henry Moore,
Court of the Macgowan Theater, UCLA

Class in Scuba Diving, Santa Barbara

Santa Barbara

At Santa Barbara, the low promontory on which the campus stands juts southward into the sea. From the beaches along its sides one can watch the sun and moon rise, as well as set, over the Pacific. Behind the coastal cliffs lies a lagoon maintained as a wildlife refuge, with a marine laboratory at its eastern end. A few miles away rise the rugged Santa Ynez Mountains, and beyond them the Santa Ynez Valley and the vast Los Padres National Forest. This proximity of sea, mountain, and rugged wild area has incited a strong interest in biology and ecology.

Several of Santa Barbara's other major dedications stem from its history. Initiated by Bostonians, it began in 1891 as a private school to train young women in manual arts and crafts, including cookery, according to the methods of the Swedish educational reformer, Otto Salomon. The city of Santa Barbara and then the state of California took over its support, and it became a normal school of manual arts and home economics, the first in the United States to train teachers in these subjects. The first male student enrolled in 1911. Through various transmutations the school became a teachers college and then a state college. In 1944, it became a campus of the University of California.

In 1949, the University acquired the promontory near Goleta, which had served as a United States Marine Corps Air Base during World War II; Santa Barbara College moved from its crowded city campus to the new site in 1954, the wartime barracks serving as offices, residences, classrooms, laboratories, and workshops while construction of the new buildings proceeded. Santa Barbara had hoped to remain essentially a small and intimate college devoted to the arts, humanities, and sciences, but in 1958 the Regents announced it must now become a general campus of the University and prepare for an eventual enrollment of fifteen thousand. And through this "uncomfortable, inconvenient, soul-shaking transformation from a single college to a university campus," as Vernon I. Cheadle, chancellor, said, "we do envision more nearly a large liberal arts college atmosphere than do most universities."

In 1967, a far-reaching new academic plan was approved by the Regents for the Santa Barbara campus, authorizing the increase in the maximum enrollment to twenty-five thousand, to be reached in 1986, and adding several new schools and colleges as well as additional research centers.

Architecture at Santa Barbara is oriented to the views of mountains and of ocean. Palms and olives have been planted against the cinnamon-colored walls. The mild climate has encouraged the contemporary use of themes from the strong Spanish heritage of the community: open stairways lead to the roof and the sky, balconies abound, and there are many patios offering sun or shade as desired. Certain workshops, such as sculpture and theater arts, open onto terraces overlooking the lagoon, and in the Music Building area, there is a small Music Bowl, ringed with steps, where at noon and in the evening one may listen to the brass choir or a string quartet, or a chorale given by the music faculty and students.

Honor Student, Santa Barbara

Concert in the Music Bowl, Santa Barbara

The Lagoon, Speech and Drama Building, and Arts Building, Santa Barbara

"The everlasting strength of this campus, its sign of greatness, its chief ultimate goal will be its ceaseless determination to be free to seek the truth and to extend the truth, to think and speak boldly, to find courage to have all sides aired before it, to stand dedicated to the cause of freedom and justice in our country and everywhere. If UCSB lives up to those traditions of free universities, if it gathers together and nourishes great scholars, all else that is good will come to it."

VERNON I. CHEADLE
Chancellor, Santa Barbara

The new Electrical Engineering Building, Santa Barbara

Santa Barbara Seniors who attended the
Universities of Madrid, Spain, and
George August, Goettingen, Germany

Bulletin Board, Education Abroad, Santa Barbara

The Education Abroad Program, administered for the University through Santa Barbara, enables qualified juniors and seniors to spend a full academic year at one of fourteen partner universities on three continents. Among these are the University of Padua, founded in 1222, where Copernicus studied and Galileo taught; the University of Edinburgh, founded in 1583, renowned for its excellence in literature, medicine, and theology; and George August University in Goettingen, founded in 1737 and now a world center in the study of mathematics and physics.

Other well-known host universities are Bordeaux, Madrid, Lund (Sweden), St. Andrews (Scotland), the University of Birmingham, and the University of Sussex (England), the International Christian University (Mitaka-Tokyo), the Chinese University of Hong Kong, the Hebrew University of Jerusalem, and the Weizmann Institute, the American University of Beirut, and the University of the Andes in Bogotá (Colombia). The primary purpose of the program is to provide a sound academic experience in a different educational system. The study centers also enable the University of California students to become deeply involved in the language and culture of the host country.

Sign in the Bookshop, Santa Barbara

Class Change, Riverside

Riverside

The Citrus Experiment Station, set on the mountain slopes above Riverside in 1907 by the University to help the young citrus industry, was world-famous, visited by hundreds of scientists, and receiving graduate and postdoctoral students from many nations, when in 1948 the University decided to build "an ideal small college of liberal arts" on one of its flanking slopes—not, as at Davis, an undergraduate College of Agriculture to which the station could extend its profound knowledge of citrus and of arid lands, but, illogically, a little college that wanted nothing more than friendly relations and an occasional lecture. In fact, the cadre of distinguished scholars and administrators who were organizing it, each of whom had been "minutely trained in a single academic discipline for the degree of Doctor of Philosophy," were deliberately avoiding specialization. "Perhaps," said the first provost, Gordon S. Watkins, a Welsh-born economist who had recently resigned as dean of letters and science at Los Angeles because he longed to get back to research and teaching, "it was because we were so familiar with the cultural limitations of specialization that we were so eager to escape its narrowing effects."

"The ideal small college of liberal arts," proposed by Robert Gordon Sproul, dynamic and persuasive president of the University for nearly thirty years, was one of the University's early attempts to solve the problems of specialization. Most great universities during the fractionalization of knowledge, had become a babel of scholarly and scientific languages often incomprehensible, even to full professors in other fields, and totally bewildering to the undergraduate wandering down below these muezzin voices. The desire for coherence, the need for unity, felt throughout the world in the arts of sciences, led professors and administrators to examine anew what were the educational needs of any individual in the complex contemporary world. As one answer, educators were recommending a broad cultural foundation and believing it best acquired in small colleges.

Arches, Humanities Building, Riverside

But universities, like glaciers, accumulate enormous force from the past, and shape through sheer weight the submerged intellectual landscape. To change the course of a glacier or a university requires a powerful obstacle, or a change of climate. "The ideal small college" was an attempt to change the climate.

The Korean War delayed construction at Riverside. When finally the college opened, in a downpour, in February, 1954, there were four broad divisions: humanities, life sciences, physical sciences, and social sciences.

it to expand. In 1959, the Regents announced that Riverside must now become a general campus of the University "continuing its undergraduate and Citrus Experiment Station functions, and expanding when appropriate into other areas that are within the sphere of the University, including graduate, professional, and organized research work." The idea of a small college within a university persisted, to emerge most strikingly in the academic plans for Santa Cruz and San Diego. At Riverside itself, the tradition of excellence in education continued as it added departments, and its graduate division, one eighth of whose students came from foreign countries, increased annually about twenty-four percent.

Its august neighbor up the hill also expanded; renamed by the Regents the Citrus Research Center and Agricultural Experiment Station, it has become the headquarters and center of the University-wide Division of Agricultural Sciences for Southern California. A college of Agriculture was established in 1961. At Riverside, now a united campus, there were founded the nationally important Air Pollution Research Center and the Dry Lands Research Institute international in scope, with the unique Philip L. Boyd Desert Research Center in nearby Deep Canyon.

Physics Major, Riverside

Within four years, because of its high standards and the superior students it attracted, Riverside became known as "the Amherst of the West." But it could not remain small; the pressures of increasing population from without, and the desire of both faculty and students to pursue graduate work from within, forced

FM Radio Station KUCR, Hans Wynholds, Manager, Riverside

When KUCR went on the air for the first time, on Sunday, October 2, 1966, at 2:00 P.M., it was the climatic moment of nearly two years' hard work. Only three of the original band of student enthusiasts remained; the rest had graduated. Cooperation from the students, faculty, and administration of UCR had throughout been instant and generous: the Associated Students promised an annual operating budget; the Regents contributed ten thousand dollars to build and equip the station; Chancellor Ivan Hinderaker and the business manager, Chuck O'Neil, helped find the station a home—in half of a married student's duplex, out of which two soundproofed and air-conditioned studios were made; the city of Riverside donated a sixty-foot steel tower for the antennae; visits to local professional stations as well as other university-operated stations, such as KAL at Berkeley, KCSB at Santa Barbara, and KZSU at Stanford, led to improvements in knowledge and acquisitions of equipment which might need a little work, but was well worth it. The delays came from the FCC, which kept putting off granting the license and construction permit for nearly a year. And the call letters, KUCR, appeared to belong to a ship radio station of a banana freighter in the Caribbean. Research on the history of this ship eventually revealed that having been sold to another nation, she was now using a different call signal. So KUCR could go on the air identifiably and appropriately as a station owned by the Regents of the University of California and operated by the students of the University at Riverside.

KUCR serves as an educational facility enhancing communication between UCR and the community of Riverside, and stations operated by students at other campuses. Arts, languages, events, forums, and special talents of faculty, students, and visitors are integral to its programs, live or taped. Music of widely varying types not broadcast by nearby stations is, of course, its mainstay, and each disc jockey is responsible for the selection he lends or borrows; the station hopes to acquire eventually an outstanding collection of records. The major presentation on KUCR's first broadcast was the dedication ceremony and first concert of the great carillon bell tower.

"The student was our central focus. It was not enough, we believed, to develop and sharpen the average mind and provide a wide latitude of freedom for the exceptional mind; we desired, also, to turn out men and women of refined manners, possessing compulsive urges to creative living, conscious of the need for constructive service to the nation and mankind, and sensitive to the imperative necessity for moral and spiritual values in a confused, disorganized and belligerent civilization."

GORDON S. WATKINS
Provost Emeritus, Riverside

The Carillon, Riverside

A magnificent musical instrument and one capable of great versatility, the carillon serves as a symbol at the heart of student life much as does the campanile with its chime of twelve bells at Berkeley. Cast in France by a family who have been bell-founders for six generations, and tuned with exquisite precision, the forty-eight bells cover a range of four chromatic octaves, from the Bourdon, pitch C^1, weight 5,091 pounds, to No. 48, C^5, weight 28 pounds. The Bourdon, which bears the University seal, is known as the Centennial Bell.

History Class, Riverside

Robert V. Hine, Associate Professor of History and Chairman of the Department, conducts an undergraduate class in The American West in his living room.

San Diego

Alone of the new campuses, San Diego began at the graduate level. The Scripps Institution of Oceanography, down by the beach at La Jolla, world famous and world-exploring, was in another of its phases of explosive brilliance. Major research laboratories were being built nearby. Recruiting scientists of the first rank as faculty and attracting graduate students who soon joined the faculty as equals were in the tradition at Scripps. The then current director, Roger Revelle, brilliant oceanographer and charismatic leader, and his colleagues went forth seeking nothing less than the superlative in faculty. They descended on campuses all over the country, invited likely candidates for a lecture or a consultancy at La Jolla, spread out before them the opportunity of helping to create an ideal university for the Twenty-first Century while living on cliffs beside the sea in a benign climate, and humbly, incessantly, asked, "How can we make it better?"

Among the earliest to respond to this dream were Nobel Laureate Harold C. Urey and Maria Goeppert Mayer, who was to receive the Nobel Prize in 1963. Many others came to be with them. The faculty thus assembled when the Graduate School of Science and Engineering was launched in 1959 was of a distinction seldom paralleled in the history of new universities. Recruitment of distinguished faculty members continued under Herbert York, who became chancellor in 1961, and John S. Galbraith, who was appointed chancellor in 1964.

The University acquired, partly from the United States Marine Corps and partly from old Spanish land grants held by San Diego, most of the long mesa that rose from the beach and continued north through groves of eucalyptus trees. Another parcel of more than 100 acres of private property was acquired in this area in 1967, making a total of 1,069 acres on which colleges for 27,500 students are now being planned.

The Breezeway, San Diego

Harold C. Urey, Professor of Chemistry at Large

Professor Urey received the Nobel Prize in 1934 for his discovery of deuterium, or heavy hydrogen. Since then, he has been given the most distinguished awards and medals and more than twenty honorary degrees from universities on two continents in the world of science, including the National Medal for Science from the United States. He has been elected to membership of the Royal Society, London, and its sister societies in Ireland, Sweden, Belgium, Norway, France, Portugal, India, and Israel, as well as those in the United States. He taught at the Universities of Montana, Johns Hopkins, Columbia, Chicago, and Oxford before coming to California and San Diego. His fields of interest include the entropy of gases, the structure of atoms and molecules, and the chemical problems of the origin of the earth, the moon, the meteorites, and the solar system. He says: "Teaching is vital to the research scientist because it takes him back to the everlasting fundamentals. I wonder who learns more: the student or the conscientious teacher?"

Graduate Student in Chemistry, San Diego brings his small daughter to the laboratory while his wife takes her finals in English.

"We want the best research
scholars in the country,
and we want them to teach."
JOHN GALBRAITH
Chancellor, San Diego

"No new theory, no new
discovery, no new work of
art will long go unexamined
or undiscussed. It will not be
a comfortable place for those
whose minds are made up."
JOHN STEWART
Provost of John Muir College,
San Diego

Fountain, San Diego
The anchor, ancient symbol of hope, as well as of Scripps' ocean
past and future, was placed in the fountain by students.

The first emphasis was on science and on close
collaboration between teacher and student. The same
attitude extends into the arts and humanities: UCSD
wants a constant procession of great creative artists
in music, painting, sculpture, dance, and theater
coming to live and work here on new ideas and
experimental forms. It encourages its scholars in the
humanities to explore the less known periods and
cultures. It expects its undergraduates—the first class
entered in 1964—as well as its graduates to initiate
projects and carry learning into their daily living.

Eventually San Diego will consist of twelve colleges
clustering together in groups of three or four, each
housing some 2,300 to 2,500 students, and each
different in architecture and dedication. It envisages
an aerial tramway down the cliff to Scripps, and, for
its central focus, not a campanile nor a carillon, but a
powerful communications tower 360 feet high,
through which to reach not only other campuses, but
also Scripps ships at sea and satellites in orbit.

"The West was ever the direction of the future! And the University of California was meant to face the future if ever a university was!"
ARCHIBALD MACLEISH

"This was precisely the spirit in which this experimental campus was launched and which we hope will sustain it through the great tasks that still lie ahead.

"We must build a unique kind of federalism by finding the proper balance of functions between the campus and the colleges. We must see each new college as a fresh chance to experiment with a new emphasis; all will be liberal arts colleges, but some in the future may be problem-oriented. We must search for original approaches to graduate life and learning, remembering as we do so how high a proportion of graduate and professional students are married and have families. We must develop better criteria than grade-point averages for selecting students from among the many qualified applicants who seek admission. We must find the best ways of culling out those who do not take advantage of what is, in effect, an honors program available to all.

"It is a fine dream, but it is more than that. We would not be here today if we did not believe that it is capable of being realized, that it is within our reach if we only have the wit and the skill and the patience to grasp it."

DEAN E. MCHENRY
Chancellor, Santa Cruz
Inaugural Address, May 3, 1966

Santa Cruz

The University of California at Santa Cruz looks down over wide pastures to the city of Santa Cruz and beyond, to the great crescent of Monterey Bay and the Pacific. Cattle still graze among the weathered fences. Some of the buildings of the old Cowell Ranch still stand, recalling a way of life rapidly vanishing from California, while others have been converted to university purposes: one barn is the beginning of a theater, and another has been transformed into a sculpture studio. The Upper Quarry, where limestone was once quarried for commercial purposes, is in the first stages of adaptation for use as an amphitheater.

Up behind the crest of the hills, in among the redwood clumps which spring up around the giant stumps of a virgin forest, a stirring experiment in education has begun: to combine, in a magnificent natural setting, the best of the small college and the best of a great university. Clustering around such central services as the University Library, the science buildings, and administration building, there will rise, about one to a year, some twenty small residential colleges, each averaging six hundred student members and forty faculty fellows, with classrooms, library, dining hall, residence houses, faculty studies, guest quarters for distinguished visitors, and a house for the provost and his family nearby.

Each college will be dedicated to the liberal arts, but will emphasize a sector of learning or a problem: Cowell College emphasizes the humanities; Adlai E. Stevenson College, the modern social sciences; Crown College, the natural sciences and mathematics.

Library, Santa Cruz

First Registration Day, 1965, Santa Cruz
". . . the unmistakable noise of students in the air."

Fountain, Santa Cruz

Other colleges will center on international studies, the fine arts, and other general fields. Student members are chosen to achieve a balanced diversity of background, ability, and interest; fellows and preceptors represent all principal disciplines in the arts and sciences, with a weighting toward the interest of the college. Not more than half the members of any college major in its field; any student may major in any discipline he chooses.

Lick Observatory is now operated from Santa Cruz, which offers a graduate program in astronomy. Other graduate and professional schools and research institutes are being added from year to year.

In these communities of intellect, contact between student and teacher is close; they live, work, and often play together. Classes are held wherever the weather and the spirit suggest, out under the redwoods perhaps, or in a sunny corner of the courtyard, or some favorite perch looking down at the Pacific. The effect is that of a cluster of hilltop villages, each with spectacular views from its windows and a square or park in its center, and each a moment's walk through a forest to its neighbor, all of which are actually parts of a great city, a great institution of learning.

The experiment has inspired gifted teachers to come from all over the country, attracted by the academic balance given teaching and research. And every year three times as many students apply as can be accommodated. By 1990, Santa Cruz expects to have an enrollment of between eighteen and twenty-five thousand.

*San Gabriel Mountains rise above the Fine Arts and
Humanities-Social Science Buildings, Irvine*

Irvine

The University of California, Irvine, was planned from the beginning to be the center of a new city of 200,000 inhabitants which is rising simultaneously, together with the industries a university attracts, according to a master plan for the whole area. The vast Irvine Ranch, 90,000 acres of open land, had been kept intact since the 1860's, when it was assembled from three Spanish land grants by James Irvine. Some of it was used for sheep and cattle, some for citrus groves, and much of it, a mountain wilderness, not at all. Finally the heirs decided to develop the ranch as a regional whole, and hired to design it William J. Pereira, architect and urban planner, whose projects already embraced a variety of institutions and communities in Southern California, as well as New England, Hawaii, and Africa. When the Regents of the University of California asked him to help them find a campus site in Southern California, he led them to twenty-three different possibilities, ending with his own favorite, the noble uplands of the Irvine Ranch, which look forth on a panoramic sweep of mountains to the north and east and down to a marsh full of wildlife on the west. The Regents agreed. The Irvine Ranch donated a thousand acres for the site and the Regents purchased another five hundred.

Pereira, whose research into the idea, role, and function of the University led him back to Athens, Alexandria, and the huge universities of medieval Europe, believes: "The university is the most important invention of the west." He also believes that in a new community, such as Berkeley a hundred years ago and Irvine now, each student means four new jobs, and each job means six new people. A university thus becomes a dynamic population center. The Irvine campus, the only one to be designed by a single architectural firm, is shaped like a giant wheel, the spokes being quadrangles ranged along pedestrian malls, with a park, eventually to have a carillon tower, as its hub.

All major buildings rise from strong horizontal bases created by terraces, heavy piers, and platforms; the malls and stairs connecting them at various levels

were all conceived and executed as an integral part of the monumental use of light and space suggested by the rolling, rising hillsides. So was the colossal landscape project developed for this treeless place—formal settings for buildings and malls; tree-shaded walks; the naturalistic central park with its (eventually) great trees, glades, and rock outcroppings; and groves along the canyons leading up to majestic silhouettes upon the hilltops. Furthermore, it would be an arboretum on campus, of the many and magnificent trees, shrubs, and other forms which are native to the subtropic "Mediterranean" climate throughout the world. Seeds and cuttings from West Australia, the Cape of Good Hope, and Chile, as well as from the Mediterranean and California itself were germinated and rooted at UCLA hothouse and mist-house facilities, and an exquisite "plant palette" developed for the whole campus. Gifts of whole groves are given, and Arbor Day will become an annual event.

William Pereira, master planner and architect
for the Irvine campus.

55

Science Lecture Hall,
Natural Science Building, Irvine

Most of the year, the skies above Irvine are white with haze or high fog, and the glare under the hot sun becomes intense. Unshaded glass and blank walls would be intolerable. Forms of precast concrete, some as simple as a long convex shield, have been devised for each quadrangle group, and fitted together to provide a daylong play of shadows over the walls, as well as hoods and shields for windows through which it is a pleasure to look out at the mountains and the hills, and at the University and the community being erected among them.

Students on veranda of the
Humanities-Social Science Building, Irvine

The academic plan for Irvine called for the shortest and most effective means of converting gifted high school students into enlightened citizens prepared for their responsibilities in whatever role or profession they choose. Undergraduates at Irvine can, with a faculty adviser, literally write their own program. If they can pass an examination in a certain subject, they don't have to take the course. If they produce something original and important, they are given credit for it. They are encouraged, in subjects apart from their major, to take courses in widely different departments on a pass-fail basis, in order that they understand the civilization they are about to enter on as broad a basis as possible. They also make their own rules of conduct in the residence cottages.

Drama Student at Irvine

Campus Park, The Commons, and Library Administration Building, Irvine

The Doe Library, Berkeley

LIBRARIES

From the College of California, the young University inherited about 1,200 volumes, which were stored in an attic and open to students for exactly one hour a day. No whispering or tobacco-chewing was allowed. At a signal from the librarian, all books were returned to him at five o'clock precisely. Yet for at least one student in those early years, "What wonders that little library contained!" Thirty years later Josiah Royce, the eminent philosopher, could recall: "I spent in the alcoves of that garret some of the most inspiring hours of my life. . . . There are books still on the shelves of our University Library here which I can look upon as among the dearest friends of my youth."

The position of librarian, with three hundred dollars monthly, in gold, was offered in 1870 to Bret Harte, who declined, and a full-time librarian was not appointed until 1875. Joseph Cummings Rowell, '74, was not a trained librarian, but for forty-four years, he continued to approach with energy and originality the many problems of his rapidly expanding library. When he began, it had grown to more than 14,000 volumes, and was already crowding its quarters in old South Hall. The gift by Henry Douglas Bacon of $25,000 toward a new library building, together with his personal library and art collection, was matched by the legislature. In 1881, the library was moved into Bacon Hall, where at first there seemed so much space that the viticulture division of the College of Agriculture used its basement as a wine cellar. Fifteen years later, in accordance with the architectural plan for the expansion of the entire campus made possible by Phoebe Apperson Hearst, Rowell was proposing a library building to accommodate 750,000 volumes and 1,000 readers, connected by subway and a "pneumatic book railway" with other buildings. This did not materialize, and the purchase of the Bancroft Library, together with Mrs. Hearst's many gifts of essential items in art and architecture, rare books and manuscripts, increased the pressure for more space. A munificent bequest by Charles Franklin Doe, plus a state bond issue, resulted in the Doe Memorial Library, designed by John Galen Howard, which from 1911 to the present day has served as the Main Library of the Berkeley campus.

The Lawrence Clark Powell Library, Los Angeles

In 1945, when Donald Coney became University Librarian, Berkeley's holdings totaled 1,260,504 volumes; in 1955, it reached the two million mark, and the Crocker family presented it with a Shakespeare First Folio to commemorate the event. Today, in addition to the main library, there are on campus twenty-three special libraries serving the five colleges, the ten schools, the many research institutes, and programs of study. Among university libraries in the United States, Berkeley ranks first in research and sixth in size; in strength and distinction, it is surpassed only by Harvard University and the Library of Congress.

The library which the "Southern Branch" of the University inherited in 1919 from the Los Angeles State Normal School was totally inadequate even for a beginning university; it did not have a single scholarly edition of Chaucer or Shakespeare, nor had it yet subscribed to the *Oxford English Dictionary.* Valiant battles to improve and strengthen it were fought over the years by its librarians. John E. Goodwin insisted from the first that it be built not only to supply the needs of undergraduates, but to become the foremost library in southern California, capable of meeting every demand that might be made upon it. Under Lawrence Clark Powell, his successor, the library grew by more than a million volumes, and provided new subject collections for major new schools of engineering, medicine, law, nursing, social welfare, business administration, and library service, and for programs in Oriental languages, theater arts, folklore, journalism, and Latin American, African, and Near East studies. When Powell retired to become dean of the School of Library Service, Robert Vosper was chosen to head the next great period of expansion. In 1964, the library acquired its two millionth volume, and rose to rank of eleventh in the nation. That same year, it opened its new Research Library. In addition to this and the Main Library, there are fifteen special libraries on campus. More than 150,000 volumes are added to the libraries annually.

Main Library, Davis

In biology and the agricultural sciences, pomology, apiculture, animal husbandry, veterinary science, enology, and gastronomy, Davis possesses collections rarely surpassed anywhere. To these, many more are being added, such as the Atomic Energy Commission Depository Library, fine collections of the periods of Milton and Wordsworth, and steadily growing collections in the arts and museology.

In December, 1960, Melvin J. Voigt, now University librarian at San Diego, suggested that identical undergraduate libraries for the three future campuses at Irvine, Santa Cruz, and San Diego, all scheduled to open in 1964 or 1965, be purchased and processed in triplicate simultaneously. A basic list of 75,000 to 80,000 volumes would follow the general size and subject balance of the successfully working Lamont Library at Harvard University and the Undergraduate Library at the University of Michigan. The Regents approved, and the bibliographies of each field were subjected to searching review by graduate librarians with experience of college libraries. Their suggestions were then scrutinized by specialists in each main field. In the final list, many times revised, books were selected for their excellence and relevance alone, irrespective of availability. About a third of the titles were out of print; when advertisement failed to find them, orders were placed with a dealer with worldwide connections. All processing was done at San Diego, where a distinguished graduate library was already operating. The other librarians were thus free to concentrate on building collections that would be needed when their graduate and research programs were initiated.

The rising costs of books were offset by discounts in price and the reduction of processing costs. On opening day, 90,000 volumes awaited the first undergraduate class at Santa Cruz, 80,000 at San Diego, and nearly 100,000 at Irvine. Faculties received the "instant libraries" with unqualified enthusiasm. Because of worldwide interest, the list has been published with the cooperation of the American Library Association and the Library of Congress.

The total number of volumes on all the University's campuses is now rapidly approaching 8,000,000. Campus libraries are connected by teletype and data-processing systems, not only to each other, but to special research libraries. Daily intercampus bus services run between Berkeley, Davis, and Santa Cruz in the north, and Los Angeles, Santa Barbara, Riverside, Irvine, and San Diego in the south.

Reading Room, San Diego

University Librarian, Santa Cruz

Donald T. Clark surveys his library, with its glass-walled court, and balconies open to the air which look out into the surrounding redwoods.

William Blake's
The Book of Job,
Fine Arts Collection,
San Diego

*The Plate of Brass, claiming California for England, which
Sir Francis Drake posted on the shores of Marin County
in 1579. Bancroft Library, Berkeley.*

Special Libraries

In 1859, Hubert Howe Bancroft, San Francisco book-seller and stationer, began collecting books and manuscripts for what was to be his thirty-nine-volume history of western North America. A pioneer in what is now called "oral history," he sent his agents throughout the state to collect dictations and memoirs from the early pioneers. He expanded his collection into newspapers, maps, and federal and state documents, and his purchase of the Andrade Collection of Mexicana laid the basis for the library's Hispanic holdings. In 1905, he sold his library to the University of California.

Greatly augmented and expanded, especially during the directorship of George P. Hammond, the Bancroft surpasses the other major collections in its manu-script resources: it now contains more than four million journals, diaries, and other personal and business papers concerned with the history of North America, from Alaska to Panama and from the Rockies to Hawaii. Its visual resources include such famous objects as the Drake Plate, the Wimmer Nugget, the Codex Fernandez Leal, a pictograph scroll of Mayan battles in Guatemala, and the magnificent Honeyman Collection of Early Californian and Western American Pictorial Material, with its more than two thousand items ranging from oils and watercolors to photographs, maps, sheet music, and posters.

Gifts of rarities and unique collections and bequests and purchases of outstanding private libraries have enriched the libraries on every campus of the University. Some, like that of C. K. Ogden, originator of Basic English and a man of omnivorous interests, were distributed among the campuses according to need. Others have been kept intact and specially housed, like the Elmer Belt Library of Vinciana at UCLA, which includes facsimiles of all Leonardo's drawings, and manuscripts and original editions of books that were his source of learning. The William Andrews Clark Memorial Library, the first great gift

the Los Angeles Library received, occupies a charming Renaissance-style building surrounded by formal lawns and gardens, about ten miles from the Los Angeles campus; its collections are particularly rich in the literature and music of seventeenth and eighteenth century England, Wildeiana, and fine printing from Gutenberg to the present day.

The Wimmer Nugget, found in Sutter's millrace, which started the Gold Rush, is here displayed in gold scales of the period. Bancroft Library, Berkeley.

The Mark Twain Collection

Professor of English Henry Nash Smith considers with Frederick
Anderson, librarian in charge of the Mark Twain Collection,
which of the manuscripts, letters, and records in the eleven four-
drawer filing cases at Berkeley should be published next. Three
books, the first of perhaps fifteen in a special series, have already
been drawn from this archive. Several previous works were
edited or written by Smith, leading scholar of the phenomenon
Samuel Clemens, who called himself after the leadsmen's call
in the Mississippi River, *Mark Twain.*

The Humanists

Great libraries, discerning special collections, and gifted scholars are reciprocals, each building up the other to fresh directions in the study of humanity.

Department of English, Berkeley

Professor of English and chairman of the department, James D. Hart stands beside shelves testifying to the current productivity of members of the department. Of his own works, undoubtedly the most widely known is the invaluable *Oxford Companion to American Literature*. Of his *The Popular Book: A History of America's Literary Taste*, Henry Steele Commager wrote ". . . one of the most entrancing volumes of literary criticism of our time. Hart is a pioneer in the field; he is immensely learned in things that most scholars disdain; he writes with clarity and vivacity and humor." In *American Images of Spanish California*, he studied the attitudes of Americans toward the Spanish and Mexican culture in California.

Center for Medieval and Renaissance Studies, UCLA

Lynn White, Jr., professor of history, pioneer researcher into the technology of the Middle Ages, and president of Mills College from 1943 to 1958, sits in the Sculpture Court of UCLA with two esteemed colleagues, Gustave von Grunebaum, Islamist, director of the UCLA Near Eastern Center, and Milton Anastos, professor of Byzantine Greek.

"Very largely for their own delight," according to Lynn White, founder of the center, some eighty humanists of UCLA are gathered together in the center to consider afresh in the light of a different century such achievements as those of Galileo and Gibbon.

New Methods of Learning

Television and the computer have been developed into means through which the great teacher can reach beyond one classroom or lecture hall and simultaneously address thousands, even millions, of students—and not just once, but again and again, as he is needed. Into the making of a videotaped course, he can bring not only the immediacy of his presence but whatever he chooses from the immense visual and aural resources of today. Into the programming of a "teaching machine" he can put all that teachers have learned about teaching since Socrates, whose dialogue is the essential principle of the teaching machine. The computer as a teaching device can go beyond the Socratic dialogue and give the student himself the

Televised Instruction, Santa Barbara

Edward L. Triplett, associate professor of biology, points out and describes the microscope image via closed-circuit television to hundreds of students simultaneously in many small class-rooms. Many of these lecture demonstrations are video-taped for future reference. In this "fundamentals of biology" course, such instruction is given four times a week and followed up in each class-room with discussions led by a graduate student. The televised films, slides, and the *realia* of biology are further supplemented by laboratory group meetings.

capability of discovering new knowledge and simultaneously projecting it to applied problems.

The University of California, under pressure within and without from the knowledge and population explosions, was a pioneer among the explorers of these potentials. Computers for data processing were set up at both Berkeley and UCLA by November, 1956; seven campuses now possess computer centers. The UCLA Western Data Processing Center, originally serving the Graduate School of Business Administration, has grown until it serves more than a hundred colleges and universities, from the University of Alaska to the University of Mexico, from the Air Force Academy in Colorado to the University of Hawaii. Data dial-phoned into several computer centers is scheduled in Los Angeles by one computer for processing by the huge central IBM 7094. Computations which performed manually might take weeks or months are concluded in seconds. But data processing is only the simple "yes or no" beginning of the potentials to which imaginative and gifted engineers, psychologists, teachers, and many others are developing the powerful and versatile computer. With a patience and a skill beyond any but the rarest living teacher, a computer can interest a child with emotional or learning problems, and at his own pace, at his convenience, bring him to excited involvement with learning and communicating. Advanced audio-instructional technique allows a language student interested in Japanese, Russian, Swahili, Urdu, or any of the 127 languages living and dead taught in the University to dial in from a remote carrel to the "audio-library" and listen to native speakers at the level of learning required; then the student can record his own attempts and play both back to compare. Language instruction by such devices has immensely aided rapid, fluent, accurate, and idiomatic mastery of such languages and dialects as the Peace Corps requires.

The architect and the engineer can, through computers, project a structure as yet only in the mind, turn it through all dimensions, alter and improve it, and hold it several hours for discussion.

There is no substitute for the living presence of the great teacher. But today there is no substitute for what the computer and television together enable him to do.

Linguistics, Santa Barbara

Linguistics includes the study of electronic speech and its modulation. Here in the speech laboratories of the Santa Barbara Campus, Pierre Delattre, professor of French, uses artificial speech synthesizers to study the acoustic elements which make vowels and consonants intelligible. With these machines, hand-painted patterns of speech can be transformed into clear sounds and manipulated at will to observe the effect of changes upon the ear.

Electrical Engineering, Santa Barbara

Graduate student working in computer theory and design examines one of the circuitry panels used in a program of computer science.

The Lawrence Hall of Science, Berkeley

High on Charter Hill at Berkeley, on a promontory looking down over the University to the Golden Gate, there are rising, stage by stage, bold crystalline shapes of concrete and glass that will eventually culminate in a huge domed star. The purpose of the Lawrence Hall of Science is as dynamic as its architecture: it is a national center for continuing research in science education at all levels and for all audiences. It is answering a national need for scientific literacy.

Science, especially during the last decades, has skyrocketed out of the layman's comprehension. Astounding discoveries and revolutionary new concepts crowd the headlines; even adults with a reasonably good education are bewildered. For the young in elementary and secondary schools where science education has often been dull and superficial, the result has been apathy; few are moved to meet the challenge and excitement of science.

To combat this apathy, many educators have experimented with television courses, tapes and movies, popular paperbacks and magazine articles, exhibits, and programmed visual devices. Some are excellent—clear, dramatic, and stimulating; many more have failed because their makers lacked experience with the necessary techniques.

For Harvey E. White, professor of physics at Berkeley and now director of the Lawrence Hall of Science, the most immediate need was to teach the teachers. A daring and ingenious innovator in science education himself, he has taught physics at Berkeley since 1930. To bring the excitement of science from the laboratory to the classroom, he developed new courses and techniques, and wrote a dozen textbooks which have sold over a million copies.

When two surveys made during the early 1950's revealed the appalling state of science education in the high schools, White decided to take action. In 1956, he taught on television a physics course to forty-four high schools in the Pittsburgh area of Pennsylvania, and in 1958, gave the first nationwide telecast of a college physics course for credit—an achievement for which he received nine national television awards.

That same year, Ernest O. Lawrence died. The Regents and Glenn Seaborg, then chancellor at Berkeley, began planning a hall of science as a memorial to this great scientist.

With the appointment of White as its first director in 1959, the Lawrence Hall of Science began to materialize as a research center in science education, supported in part by national agencies, foundations, and private donors.

While it was being built, White and an imaginative and inventive staff worked on teaching aids: for elementary schools, science kits— portable cases containing preserved animal specimens which the children can handle; for high schools, model laboratory classrooms whose components are now being made nationally available; for large classes, an amphitheatre where each student teacher has his own table television receiver; for exhibition areas, devices that attract students to play with them—for instance, pinball machines demonstrating the principle of the Bevatron and the linear accelerators. Of still greater potential importance are devices through which experiments can be performed even at college level.

Construction, The Lawrence Hall of Science, Berkeley

Harvey E. White, director of the Lawrence Hall of Science, and the tower of the memorial to Ernest O. Lawrence, which contains the first cyclotron, his Nobel Prize, and other accomplishments and honors of his life.

"The Hill" at Berkeley Frontiers of modern science are represented by Space Sciences Laboratory, Lawrence Hall of Science, and Lawrence Radiation Laboratory.

Much of this equipment is in use at the Lawrence Hall of Science. Teachers from all over the country, aided by scholarships, grants, and sabbatical leaves, come to its Education Center. Here, with scientists, psychologists, engineers, designers, and writers, they discuss new concepts and the most dynamic way to present them. In the model classrooms, they teach students from all ages and backgrounds; in the workshops they learn to devise and construct their own visual aids. In the television studio, the first in the United States to be fully equipped for science programs, they acquire the art of television instruction and of making videotapes. In the auditorium, which has a rotating stage and television receivers visible by every member of the audience, they perfect the arts of demonstrating and lecturing.

From the Education Center, the Visitors' Center grows naturally, as a flower from seed. Eventually there will be eight exhibit-instruction galleries radiating from the dome and cantilevered out into space. Each will be devoted to a main branch of science: astronomy, biology, geology, chemistry, physics, mathematics, nuclear science, and space science. Here the visitor can choose the level at which he wishes to participate. He can push a button and get a vivid visual demonstration, or he can go on to perform experiments with devices that permit him to test what he has learned. Many of these experiments are cumulative: for instance, in space science, he can progress through a series of exhibits on gravity, velocity, the laws of Kepler and Newton, et cetera, until, with his new knowledge of celestial mechanics and space biology, he can assist at a simulated space flight.

University Art Museum, Berkeley

An art museum for Berkeley, as has been wryly observed, has been the subject of "more talk and more procrastination" than any other project on campus. In 1927, old Bacon Hall, which had once housed the University library as well as its first art gallery, was remodeled for the Departments of Geology and Geography. The young Art Department had now no place to hang a show even of its own work. To study the art of other periods and cultures, students and faculty, as well as the rest of Berkeley community, had to take off a Saturday or Sunday and go to San Francisco.

In 1933, a faculty member and an alumnus, seizing on the obsolete steam plant which had been designed by John Galen Howard, raised enough money to convert the handsome little structure into "a temporary art museum." The result was inadequate; loan and traveling shows had to be turned down for lack of

proper facilities. Prospective donors of important works of art, seeing no place where their treasures could be properly exhibited or cared for, bestowed them elsewhere. There were already more than six thousand paintings, sculptures, and other art items, most of them discarded as tastes changed over the years, stored in the basement of the women's gymnasium.

William Randolph Hearst commissioned the great Bernard Maybeck to draw up plans for a museum of classical grandeur to be built in memory of his mother, Phoebe Apperson Hearst, greatest of all the University's many benefactors, but for some reason, possibly the Depression, it was never built, and the plans remain in the University archives.

Finally in 1957, Clark Kerr, then chancellor of the Berkeley campus, and always a champion of the creative, appointed a committee to study how an art center and museum could and should be set up. One result was that Donald Coney, the University librarian, took the bold step of opening the paneled walls of the Morrison Library for an exhibition of *German Expressionist Painting*, directed by Peter Selz, then a young professor of art at Pomona College, whose pioneering study of the subject was being published by the University Press. The effect was electric: one critic exclaimed, "The University of California has an exhibition of paintings! If the Cyclotron had been boarded up, we could not have been more surprised."

Next came the move to bring the old steam plant up to acceptable standards. Traveling exhibitions by such contemporaries as Picasso and Paul Klee came to the campus, and original exhibitions of Berkeley's own distinguished faculty began traveling across the country and abroad. Next came, in 1960, Kroeber Hall, named in honor of the late Professor Alfred L. Kroeber chairman of the Department of Anthropology from 1901 to 1946, which housed art as well as anthropology and archaeology, with a gallery devoted to each. The art gallery, named in honor of the painter Worth Ryder, a founder of the art department, shows only contemporary art.

These evidences of endeavor inspired Hans Hofmann, grateful to Worth Ryder for having brought him from Nazi Germany to teach at Berkeley, to give the University forty-five of his vivid paintings and a quarter of a million dollars for a wing to house them. That was the catalyst: the University finally announced its plans to build an art museum, costing around $4,200,000, all to come from private gifts or foundation funds, and set up a national competition for its design.

Protests immediately arose from the patrons of the three hard-pressed museums in San Francisco, all in need of expansion and improvement; what would happen if a fourth museum siphoned off so much of the available funds? The sympathetic Regents decided to defer the funding, whereupon such a clamor arose on campus from students and faculty alike, and so many letters supporting the idea came in from museum people across the country, including the directors of the three hard-pressed San Francisco museums, that the Regents finally voted to proceed. Such pyrotechnics might have daunted a newly arrived director of the prospective museum, but Peter Selz, who had come from seven years as curator of painting and sculpture at the Museum of Modern Art in New York, is a pyrotechnician himself.

Selz believes there is no substitute for contact with the actual art object. Slides, photographs, and reproductions can only extend acquaintance or serve as checks. He has inspired gifts from his many friends among collectors and artists, and hopes for funds to make the University collections rich in the art of all periods and cultures. He considers what the University already possesses in contemporary painting the finest west of Buffalo.

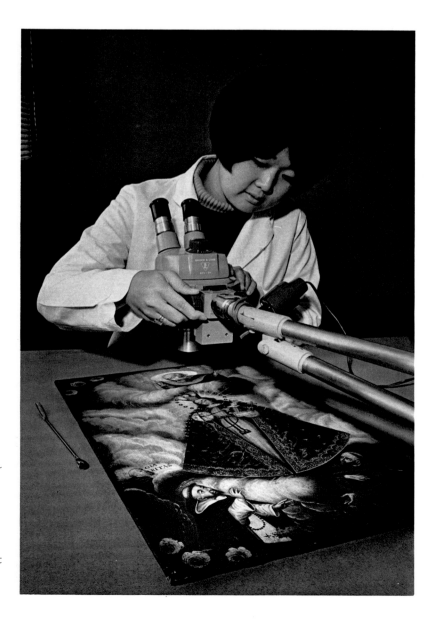

Painting Restoration, Davis

Opening in 1966, the Laboratory for Research in Fine Arts and Museology is the first school in the West where young art historians already possessing a master's degree can obtain research training in the conservation and restoration of works of art. Courses in connoisseurship which involve techniques of collecting and exhibiting are combined with actual work in the laboratory and cooperation with local museums. The laboratory emphasizes research in American art, particularly the Northwest Coast, the Southwest, and the Pre-Columbian art of Mexico and South America.

THE ARTS

"America is bursting with creativity in painting, music, literature, the theater, with a vigor equaled in few other parts of the world today. . . . In the arts, the universities have been more hospitable to the historian and the critic than the creator. . . . A very important role remains for the historian of past ages of creativity and for the critic of the current productions. But the universities need to find ways also to accommodate pure creative effort if they are to have places on stage as well as in the wings and in the audience in the great drama of cultural growth now playing on the American stage."

CLARK KERR
President of the University, 1958–1967
from *The Uses of the University*, 1963

Standing Ovation for Elektra, *Greek Theatre, Berkeley*

The Greek Theatre, gift of William Randolph Hearst in 1903, was designed by John Galen Howard. Seating ten thousand people, with space for more on the hillside above, it has served the University as a focal point for multitudes during Charter Days, Commencements, plays, and festivals, as well as orchestral and opera performances.

Today every campus of the University is the center of a cultural explosion involving not merely students and faculty, but the community and often the whole region. Yearlong, leading symphony orchestras, opera, theater, and dance companies, string quartets, great soloists, folksingers, jazz bands, film programs, exhibitions, and every kind of performance from the classic to the avant-garde, crowd the calendar of each campus, and every year the campus itself contributes more richly to the calendar its own productions in music, theater, opera, dance, film, radio, and television. Traveling art exhibitions are supplemented and extended by exhibitions from the University's own collections and of its own painters and sculptors, both faculty and student.

On every campus, too, the arts are coming out of the sheds, basements, and gymnasiums, and ceasing their migrations through buildings abandoned by more well-heeled departments. Superbly equipped theaters, art galleries, and concert halls, together with the necessary studios, workshops, and practice rooms, are being built. The presence of great creators as resident artists or as permanent members of the faculty is nothing novel; in the 1930's, at Berkeley, Hans Hofmann was teaching painting, and Roger Sessions and Ernst Bloch music, as was their fellow composer, Arnold Schoenberg, at UCLA. As faculty members, artists have full academic standing. Undergraduate art majors, in a far more exciting and demanding atmosphere than the conservatory or the atelier, may receive the A.B. degree, after completing University and college requirements, for outstanding performance or original creative work. They may continue, in several departments on various campuses, to work for the M.A. or the M.F.A. (Master of Fine Arts), the Ph.D., usually a teaching degree, or the D.F.A. (Doctor of Fine Arts). In 1963, the University took a further step: at the instigation of Clark Kerr, the Regents approved the Creative Arts Institute, whereby every year some twenty artists, usually faculty members, have the opportunity to devote a full year to their own creative work.

A performance by the San Francisco Opera Company of Elektra, *by Richard Strauss, in the Greek Theatre, Berkeley*

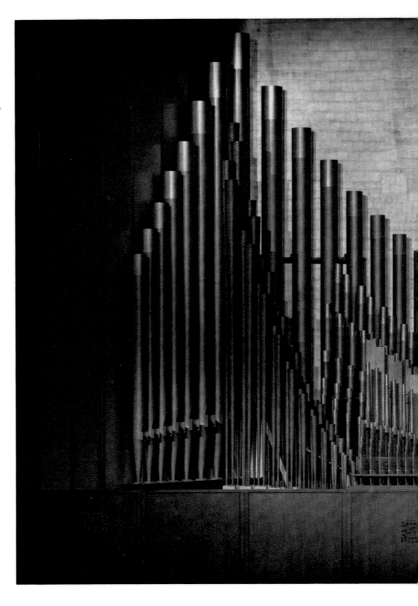

University Organist Lawrence H. Moe, professor of music and chairman of the department, at the O'Neill Memorial Organ, Hertz Hall, Berkeley.

The great concert organ, designed by Holtkamp of Cleveland, is considered by exacting critics the finest in the West. Hertz Hall, designed by Gardner Dailey, is renowned for its fine acoustics.

Music

At Berkeley, toward the turn of the century, the spontaneous—and sporadic—groups of students, faculty, and townspeople interested in music and drama were still meeting in homes or renting halls and theaters in downtown Berkeley and Oakland. Little came in from the outside. A faculty committee in 1891 sponsored the Berkeley Athenaeum "to furnish the best possible entertainment in letters, music and art to the University and to the people of Berkeley, by drawing to the University the best talent coming to the State." But they were handicapped by lack of funds and facilities. The always perceptive and generous Phoebe Apperson Hearst, who became a Regent in 1897, not only opened her home for concerts and art lectures to which students and faculty were freely invited—she established a string quartet in residence on the campus. Her son's gift of the Greek Theatre and of funds to support its programs opened a whole new world to the faculty committee: now

they could bring together—true, only in the open air and in fine weather—vast audiences with the greatest orchestras, concert bands, and artists of the day. Sarah Bernhardt, Maude Adams, Luisa Tetrazzini, Ruth St. Denis—these and many more appeared on the stage of the Greek Theatre. Ten thousand people, according to a 1906 account, attended "the Wagner Concert." By then, the legislature had acceded to the demand for a department of music, and allocated six thousand dollars "to provide for two years the salary of a Professor of Music."

That first professor, John Frederick Wolle, conducted an orchestra composed of local professional musicians at University concerts, set up the undergraduate University Symphony Orchestra and Chorus, and taught harmony, counterpoint, and choral and instrumental music. His successor, Charles L. Seeger, Jr., who came in 1912, amplified the curriculum and

the faculty. In 1916, he gave an introduction to musicology, believed to be the first ever given in the United States. Thus early was laid the foundation of what has since been built into one of, if not the most, distinguished musicological departments in the entire country. The department's strong program for composers began in the 1930's with the appointment to the faculty of such noted composers as Randall Thompson, Roger Sessions, and Ernest Bloch. Special performing groups have been formed within the basic symphonic and choral organizations, such as the Repertory Chorus, which explores unusual and early choral music, the Collegium Musicum, a group of singers and players whose performance of songs by Monteverdi and Frescobaldi have been recorded by Cambridge Records, and the Chamber Band, which presents such remarkable compositions as Stravinsky's Concerto for Piano and Wind Instruments.

Until the late 1950's, the music department led a migratory existence here and there around campus, without adequate practice and recital facilities or even office and classroom space. Then came the generous bequest of most of his fortune by the late Alfred Hertz, the beloved, bald-headed and black-bearded conductor of the San Francisco Symphony Orchestra from 1915 to 1930. Half, he stipulated, should go to maintain scholarships for talented young muscians. The other half was to erect, or help erect, a building for music. May T. Morrison made a still larger gift. The department now has not only a home, but a recital hall which has greatly enriched the musical life of the entire Bay Area. Soloists, string quartets, small operas, and unusual ensembles, chosen with discriminating care, concerts by the University organist and the various University orchestral and choral groups cause the 720 seats in Hertz Hall to be sold out well in advance of the 120 or so concerts held there each year.

Regents' Professor of Musicology, Riverside

Oswald Jonas, internationally known music theorist, came to
Riverside in 1966 as a Regents' Professor. Displaying his
collection of early scores, he urges young musicians always to
begin their study of any musical work with the composer's
original concept. Over the centuries, slight changes made by
successive editors, arrangements for instruments unknown to
the composer, and personal interpretations by great performers
and conductors have often insensibly contributed to quite
distorted contemporary approaches.

Opera

To give everyone everywhere the exciting experience of opera is a dream Jan Popper, professor of music at UCLA, is bringing closer and closer to realization. In his native Czechoslovakia he was already celebrated as a virtuoso-concert pianist, conductor, especially of Mozart, and director of highly imaginative productions of opera and musical comedy, when the threat of invasion by Nazi Germany caused him to join the air force as pilot and paratrooper. With his country crushed and its armed forces dismantled, Popper fled to England, and in 1939 came to the United States.

Here, instead of the lively interest in opera that makes the provincial opera companies of Europe the finest training ground for young singers, he found the pleasures of opera virtually unknown outside of a wealthy and musical few in large cities. The average citizen, if he had indeed attended an opera, thought it boring and, being usually in a foreign tongue, incomprehensible and slightly ridiculous. With such limited popular support, only major opera companies such as the Metropolitan, the Chicago, and the San Francisco survived the impact of the movies and television; these engaged internationally famous voices, and seldom offered room for the young and untrained, no matter how gifted. To bridge these gulfs, opera workshops—indigenous to America— were springing up at universities and conservatories in the East. Jan Popper founded, at Stanford University, the first in the West.

In 1949, Popper came to found an opera workshop at UCLA, and soon southern Californians by the hundreds found themselves becoming opera lovers, eager for the next new production. Classic or contemporary, these were always in English, and always brilliantly directed and staged. Simultaneously teacher and lecturer, often appearing as guest conductor in the Hollywood Bowl and with the San Francisco Symphony Orchestra, Popper became known and beloved up and down California as the apostle of opera. His television series, *Spotlight on Opera*, in 1955, enchanted audiences who had previously dismissed educational television as dull and incompetent.

In 1966, a further stage of Popper's dream materialized: the UCLA Opera Theater, a professional opera company formed around a nucleus of talented young singers and dancers with outstanding and widely experienced performers in the leading roles. Thanks to the unique foundation established by the will of Gladys Turk, who remembered what it was to be a young singer with a fine voice and no money for further training, substantial grants were made to some thirty recent graduates. UCLA, Berkeley, and the Intercampus Cultural Exchange Committee combined funds to help mount the new company's productions. In their first season, Kurka's *The Good Soldier Schweik*, that rollicking twentieth-century satire with its blend of Czech folktunes and American jazz rhythms, contrasted with Cimarosa's charming opera buffa, *The Secret Marriage*.

UCLA Opera Director Jan Popper, with a few of the posters and tributes from Japan.

Ethnic Arts

The civilizations of the West, though repeatedly infused by the splendor of the East, tended for centuries to be both egocentric and ethnocentric and to regard with disdain the cultures of continents which never knew the light of Greece or Rome. The objects brought back by explorers, archaeologists, and anthropologists were received as strange or "primitive," often as valueless. The dances and music seemed monotonous and dissonant. Then artists searching for new forms began to see with new eyes and hear with new ears—Debussy listening enchanted to the weird, shimmering music of a Javanese *gamelan,* Gauguin seeking the dark forms and glowing colors of the South Pacific, Picasso changing styles in mid-painting because of the dynamic and subtle forms of African Negro sculpture.

In the universities, centers for the study of Latin America, Africa, the Near East, Southeast Asia, Japan, and other geographical and ethnic regions have multiplied during the last two decades. Not only anthropologists and archaeologists, but economists, physicians, engineers, historians, folklorists, philosophers, and members of almost every discipline

have entered into the study, and none with more absorption and delight than those concerned with the arts.

By 1960, the Oriental scholars at UCLA felt they had material of such worth that it must be shared. A two-week Festival of Oriental Music and Related Arts—painting, poetry, folklore, theater, textiles, and costumes—was held, with lectures and films in the afternoons. In the evenings, costumed musicians and dancers representing Iran, India, China, Bali, Java, and Japan performed on ancient and beautiful instruments from the UCLA collection. The UCLA Performance Groups, consisting of native musicians come to study and teach in the United States, American musicians and musicologists thoroughly trained in the various traditions, and an international array of students, gave concerts on such superb instruments as UCLA's one-hundred-and-twenty-year-old Javanese *gamelan,* a large orchestra of more than seventy-five instruments, revered in its own country for its exceptional quality of sound, and known as *Khjai Mendung;* "The Venerable Dark Cloud." From this first festival sprang two new institutions, the Institute of Ethnomusicology, in 1961, and the Museum and Laboratories of Ethnic Arts and Technology, in 1963. Collections have poured in to the museum from all over the world; everything indigenous to and expressive of the arts and culture of a people interests Ralph C. Altman, the museum's director. Distinguished anthropologists and art historians from England, France, Holland, Mexico, and the United States come to participate in such lecture series as "Individual Creativity and Tribal Norms" and "Folk Arts" by University Extension. The museum has sponsored research and collecting in Venezuela, Mexico, New Guinea, India, and Thailand.

The Institute of Ethnomusicology, directed by Mantle Hood, has already been long in the field, recording in Ghana, Iran, Java, Bali, India, Japan, and elsewhere, and bringing superb musicians back to UCLA. Master drummers from Ghana, musicians and dancers from the Imperial Court of Japan, from Java, from Bali, and from all nations come to teach and to learn at UCLA.

Museum and Laboratories of Ethnic Arts and Technology, UCLA

Exhibitions have ranged from bark paintings by Australian aborigines, neolithic figurines from the Danube basin, and Plains Indian warfare, to rugs from Anatolia and Christmas as celebrated in Latin American folk art.

The Japanese Garden, UCLA

One third of an acre of steep, arid, barren hillside not worth a second glance was, in 1961, suddenly transformed. Tons of rocks, many of them from Japan, began arriving; so, in great balls of earth, did pines, deodars, cryptomerias, junipers, and dwarf maples, all mature enough to possess, by accident or design, interesting shapes. Japanese landscape architects came to direct their placement and to install among them ancient stone bridges and water basins, a pagoda more than five hundred years old, and a Buddha more than a thousand. Japanese artisans assembled a gate, a teahouse, and a shrine made in Kyoto. Created by Mr. and Mrs. Gordon Guiberson from objects collected

during journeys of thousands of miles, the garden was in 1965 given by Regent Edward W. Carter to UCLA.

Today this beautiful tranquility of pine, bamboo, and stone, threaded by the many voices of water, is studied by departments of the University, including art, architecture, botany, and theater arts. Performances of Japanese chamber music such as *sankyoku* are often given here by the Institute of Ethnomusicology. Here teacher Mitsuru Yuge plays the bamboo flute, *shakuhachi,* his wife Iku the lute-like *shamisen,* and graduate student Bonnie Wade the *koto,* an ancient form of zither.

Fundamentals of Painting, Santa Cruz

When, in the fall of 1966, this first introductory course for
interdisciplinary nonmajors was offered, half of the applicants
had to be turned away for lack of room, facilities, and instructors.
The hunger for art of students in all disciplines, especially the
sciences, outran expectation; each quarter the course was full
even before registration began. Of those accepted, some of course
were all thumbs, some quite accomplished, and some astonish-
ingly gifted, necessitating a tutorial relation with each individual.
In two hours twice a week and one seminar, the sole professor
can hardly get around to each student, let alone give him or her
all he needs and desires. In the years to come, there will be more
professors, longer studio hours, and eventually better facilities.
Meanwhile, there is the magnificent studio of all outdoors among
the redwoods, the oaks, and the wildflowers at Santa Cruz.

Fundamentals of Creative Art

Fundamentals of Form, Irvine

The purpose of this beginners' class is to inculcate a total
awareness of form, founded on accurate observation of the actual,
especially the commonplace, and continuing through experiment
with the abstract into the potentials of basic form. Here a
student measures a complex polyhedron in order to observe its
effect when reconstructed on a different scale.

Sculpture

Clay, Santa Barbara
A beginners' class works at evolving forms inspired by natural
objects such as shells and thistles.

Welding, Santa Barbara

Goggles and an acetylene torch have become as essential to the sculptor in metal as to the steamfitter and the riveter.

Casting, Davis

Tio Gambruni, assistant professor of art, supervises graduate students learning to cast in bronze and aluminum by the Renaissance process known as "lost wax." Originally the model was made of wax, which melted and was consumed by the molten metal. Now styrofoam is used instead of wax.

Theater Arts

Irvine

A rehearsal of *Oedipus Tyrannos* continues at Founders' Rock, undeterred by fog. Emphasis in the arts at Irvine is on professional commitment and centers on the studio and the performance. Eventually the arts will be housed in "a fine arts village," containing studios, workshops, practice rooms, a concert hall, a theater, and courts where performances may be held in the open air.

UCLA

The crew involved in staging a production of Jean Anouilh's *The Lark* pauses in the evening's work to pose for the photographer—and read *Variety*. Theater arts have been greatly inspired by the professional Theater Group, which is now operating out of the Music Center, in downtown Los Angeles. It is a joint venture of University Extension and the theatrical professions which annually presents six productions professionally produced, acted, and directed, from both classic and contemporary repertoires. The department, in addition to its intramural, experimental productions, also annually produces six plays, many of which have never been produced before. Macgowan Hall, first unit of the theater arts building complex to be completed, contains two superbly equipped theaters, one seating six hundred and the other two hundred, with a revolving stage, and orchestra pit which can be elevated to extend the apron, light- and sound-control rooms, and a large area for building sets. Unit 2 will contain facilities and equipment representing the most advanced thought and technology in motion pictures, radio, and television.

Davis

A performance of Arthur Miller's *The Crucible* in the octagonal Wyatt Pavilion Theater. Formerly used for judging livestock, the pavilion has been converted into a small thrust stage theater. In its New Theater Arts building, Davis has both an arena theater and a proscenium theater, both well equipped, with a large backstage area and shops for scenery and costumes. Resident professional actors are now part of the Department of Dramatic Art and sometimes there are as many as seventeen plays in various stages of production.

The Film Makers:
Motion Picture Division, Theater Arts Department, Los Angeles

In 1947, when the Motion Picture Division began, in a congeries of World War II barracks somewhat hastily converted into sound stages, cutting rooms, and projection booths, no one yet had a clear idea how to teach movie-making on a university level. A trade school would teach only specialities: only student directors would direct, only future editors would use the cutting benches, and only prospective cameramen would touch the cameras. Surely, in a university, one must take a larger view, and begin with theory, history, and science. So, for three hours a week, students looked at films and listened to history studded with reminiscences and lectures on the art and science of film. Watching instructors make films, and being allowed now and then to tackle some baby exercise like shooting an exterior or cutting an old melodrama, merely whetted their eagerness to start making their own films. A few of the more foolhardy plunged ahead, whether or not they were considered ready. They rented cameras, enlisted friends and cast and crew, worked every spare hour during daylight, and sneaked into the sound stages and cutting rooms at night.

Lyric, tragic, satiric, fantastic, sometimes violent, these first little films came from inner worlds. Often they were autobiographical, and always they were passionately felt. The faculty realized they had ringside seats to what goes on in the young.

Furthermore, these students were using film in its purest form and finding it as supple and eloquent a medium for personal expression as music or poetry. Technically, these brief little efforts were surprisingly competent; the student producers, off on their own, had learned fast and thoroughly what they had to know. The faculty concluded that the only way to learn how to make films is to make them. As teachers they might help, advise, and explain, but they must let the student make his own mistakes. Several of those early students are now on the faculty themselves, and one of their students, Colin Young, is now chairman of the Department of Theater Arts.

Through the years, the curriculum has been revised until, under the project system adopted in the fall of 1966, the student is immediately precipitated into the magic involvement with film. Having completed all University and college requirements for his A.B. degree, he is free to concentrate. He learns to handle film, to shoot, cut, see, and think in film. He studies films and their history and criticism from the film maker's point of view. And he is given a challenge: to write, direct, and edit his own film, complete with sound mix, in the ten weeks of his first quarter. On this film he will be failed or passed and graded. If it's good, it may even be among the fifteen or so the department semi-annually selects for public showing.

The beginners in Project I are divided into groups of five or so, assigned a faculty advisor, and entrusted with an 8mm camera kit, a reflector, and a tape recorder. Their films will be shot outdoors, and will make use as far as possible of natural light. Each student in turn is director for a full day's shooting, while the rest of the group serve as crew in every capacity from cameraman to grip. This challenge met, the student is ready for Project II, in which he receives one hundred dollars for expenses, uses 16mm equipment, and perhaps even works with interiors and complex lighting and camera movements. Now and then, the student may decide he needs more time with camera, or further experiment with cutting or with sound. He may wish to concentrate for a while on writing, or animation, or set design. Project III is usually on the graduate level, and the young director now has access to a wider range of professional equipment and studio resources. His stake is only five hundred dollars, but a couple of sets can easily swallow that, and the division hopes for funds that will help make these stakes more realistic. Yet this may be an important part of his portfolio when he

goes to show what he can do, so somehow he raises the extra thousand dollars or so he needs, and watches his pennies like a veteran. When he comes to do his thesis, no University financing is available, but there are fellowships and scholarships up to three thousand dollars, and, of course, the department's equipment and facilities.

The semi-annual film showings in Royce Hall have become an important event. For five or six nights, the public jams into the two thousand seats, and pays for the privilege. Often the screenings are followed by calls from Hollywood, television, and other producers, as astounded by the response as by the fact that the house wasn't papered. Then the films go on to the festivals. Many have won national and international awards.

Project III Sound Stage

The director, Aspi Irani, from Bombay, India, is in this case also the actor with the beard. The actress, a semi-professional, is doing this as a "showcase." The crew are volunteers from all three project levels, and, in the opinion of their faculty advisor, who is keeping out of the way, they are shaking down into a team like pros.

III
THE UNIVERSITY'S INVISIBLE PRODUCT, KNOWLEDGE

Lick Observatory, Mount Hamilton

Mount Hamilton, though it reaches a height of only 4,200 feet above sea level, is so steep that it seems to rise like a knife edge between immensities. To the east, it looks across the San Joaquin Valley to the huge wall of the Sierra Nevada: to the west, over the Santa Clara Valley to the Coast Range. Often there is fog breaking like the sea over the Coast Range, haze in the San Joaquin, and of late years, smog in the Santa Clara, but Mount Hamilton still rises above them, its seven domes gleaming in the light.

The idea of locating astronomical instruments in the clear air of high mountains occurred first to Sir Isaac Newton early in the eighteenth century, but not until James Lick, in 1875, selected the crest of Mount Hamilton as the site of the observatory which was to bear his name, was an observatory with a major instrument built on a mountain top.

Lick bequeathed $700,000, a quarter of his fortune, for the purchase of the land and the construction of a "powerful telescope, superior to and more powerful than any telescope yet made. . . ." He is buried in the base of the 36-inch refractor, which in its time more than fulfilled his charge. It remains one of the two largest "spyglass" telescopes in the world.

Domes of the 120-inch reflector, the 36-inch and the 12-inch refractors, Lick Observatory, Mount Hamilton

Originally, the dome of the 36-inch refractor turned and its floor rose and sank by water power; now they are powered by electricity. The image quality and the ability of this great instrument to resolve fine details are so excellent that it has been fitted for visual observation with eyepieces giving magnifications of 100 to 2,000 times. On clear nights, the moon's surface may be seen as if only 120 miles away. Through the modern photographic, spectrographic, and photometric devices built for it, the 36-inch refractor continues to be Lick's "workhorse." It has been used for mapping the moon, studying the planets, discovering over 5,000 pairs of double stars, and measuring the drift of the sun in relation to neighboring stars.

Lick Observatory has pioneered not only as the first mountaintop observatory, but also in inventing and improving many new instruments and techniques.

The Crossley reflector, gift of an English amateur astronomer in 1895, was put to such brilliant use at Lick that within a decade it demonstrated to astronomers that in the future all large telescopes should be equipped with mirrors instead of lenses. Improved and modernized, it has been used in historic investigations of the form of gaseous nebulae and galaxies, the structure and spectra of planetary nebulae, and the spectra of faint variables in young clusters of stars.

The 20-inch Carnegie Astrograph, a giant camera designed and built at Lick with funds from the Carnegie Corporation in 1937, is used for precise photographic mapping of the sky. Pairs of photographs taken fifteen years apart are projected in the star comparator: one image flicks on, the other off. The astronomer can instantly note any change or motion of stars within our galaxy.

The largest astronomical telescope yet built by public funds, the 120-inch reflector was financed during the years of its construction by the California state legislature. The slow process of grinding and polishing its huge mirror to its final precise shape was completed in the optical shops at Lick in 1959.

To ascend in the elevator that carries the astronomer up the arches of the dome to the prime focus, while the dome itself revolves and the huge instrument below not only turns but lifts, is such an experience in vertigo that the unaccustomed have been known to faint.

The astronomer begins preparations for the night's work in the afternoon, when he sees that the auxiliary apparatus he will need—photographic plateholder, spectrograph, photometer, electronic camera, or other device—is assembled and attached to his telescope. At dusk, he returns to the observatory with star identification charts, a thermos of coffee, and, in winter, warm clothes against the chill of the unheated dome. On dark, moonless nights, the precious telescope hours go to studying the faintest objects: photographing them, measuring their light, or spreading their feeble rays out into a spectrum. On moonlit nights, a powerful spectrograph analyzes the brighter stars. Observations continue until dawn. After a morning's sleep, and perhaps an hour in the darkroom processing the previous night's exposures, the astronomer prepares his campaign for the next night. Or if another observer is to take over the telescope, he returns to his office to begin analysis of his data. Computers may speed the work, but the time spent in analysis far exceeds the hours at the telescope. Even though an astronomer ordinarily spends only five to eight nights a month in observing, competition for access to telescopes is severe; there will probably never be enough great instruments.

The 120-inch reflector and its giant rival, the 200-inch reflector at Mount Palomar, have for years been the two largest telescopes in the world, and in the opinion of astronomers, the only telescopes with sufficient light-gathering power to resolve the problems currently on the frontier of astrophysical research. Now other telescopes are being built or proposed, and University of California astronomers contemplate major new instruments in their plans for the future.

The 120-inch reflector, mirror detached for re-aluminizing, Lick Observatory

Radio Astronomy Observatory, Hat Creek

Sunlight, fog, clouds, haze: these do not impede radio astronomy. Only "noise" obscures its reception of signals from space. Far from transmission lines and the multitudinous radio and electrical noises emitted by population centers, Hat Creek is considered the "quietest" valley in northern California. Surrounded by the massive Hat Creek Lava Flow, it lies in the radio "shadow" of Mount Lassen, an active volcano, to the south, and of other high mountains to the north and west.

Rising strangely, like moons among the pines and the black basaltic rocks, the two parabolic reflectors can be precisely pointed to any object in the sky, and are geared to follow it against the rotation of the earth exactly as optical telescopes do. Just as the parabolic mirror of the 120-inch telescope at Lick Observatory collects visible light and brings it to a focus where it forms an image on a photographic plate or other detector, so do the shining aluminum "dishes" of the parabolic reflectors collect radio waves and focus them on a horn, which conveys their energy into a sensitive receiver. Usually these receivers are tuned in frequency so that spectral lines originating from hydrogen atoms, OH molecules, or other gaseous components of the galaxy can be investigated. The observations are recorded on IBM cards for further reduction in the computer at Berkeley. The radio telescopes at Hat Creek are at present largely devoted to discovering more about the galaxy in one of whose spiral arms our sun is a minor star. The emission from the OH molecule in space was discovered with the 85-foot radio telescope, which has been extensively used to study this mysterious constituent of our galaxy and its intense and so-far inexplicable brilliance.

Born of the electronic age scarcely three decades ago, radio telescopes permit astronomers to "see" the universe in a new way. Already they have contributed enormously to our knowledge of the activity on the surface of the sun, of the temperatures and magnetic fields of the planets, of the form and structure of this galaxy, and of conditions within the gaseous nebulae. Perhaps their most challenging discovery is the quasars (quasi-stellar radio sources), extremely distant objects receding at high speed, which radiate many times the energy of the brightest normal galaxies. Quasars have caused astronomers to seek new sources of energy throughout the universe, sources many times more powerful than the thermonuclear energy of the stars.

Parabolic Reflectors of the Hat Creek
Radio Astronomy Observatory

The Museum of Vertebrate Zoology, Berkeley

The Museum of Vertebrate Zoology was established in 1908, when Annie Alexander offered to support such an institution for seven years, and the Regents agreed to build a temporary structure of galvanized iron to house it on the knoll south of Faculty Glade. Its first director, Joseph Grinnell, decided to concentrate the museum's initial efforts on collecting the birds, mammals, reptiles, and amphibians of the west coast of North America.

Collecting began in 1909, with field expeditions manned by staff and students systematically covering first California and then, in subsequent years, Baja California, Oregon, and beyond, until they assembled one of the finest regional collections in the world and the largest held by a university. Miss Alexander, delighted with this beginning, presented the Regents with a generous endowment, whose income was to ensure the permanence of the museum's operation.

Since 1930, the museum has been housed in a wing of the Life Sciences Building, and the steel cases containing its collections tower up through three stories. Field expeditions to all continents during the last twenty-five years have brought back significant additions. Field notes, maps, and photographs are available for study along with the animals. None of these treasures is on public display; the museum is a research institute, a library of fauna, and a major resource for undergraduates, graduates, and staff. Many doctoral dissertations are based either wholly or in part on the material stored there.

Through the years, the museum's original interest in examining the hypothesis, now widely accepted, that animal evolution is based on gradual adaptation, through mutation, to local environment has steadily expanded. Museum work now includes investigation of the behavior and all other characteristics of the living animal in its evolutionary adjustments. Natural history studies have grown to encompass ecology, population dynamics, and the factors that govern local population densities.

What in the ecosystem of the Arctic tundra causes the three-year population cycle of the brown lemmings? Why do they swarm over the countryside, devouring vegetation and overcoming all obstacles, until they reach the sea and swim out until they drown? A zoologist, a forester, and a soils scientist have gone to the Arctic to investigate. What influence do photoperiods (varying lengths of night and day) have on the reproductive cycle of an equatorial finch or sparrow? How, within a genus widely distributed, such as the flycatchers, did communication signals and patterns of habitat utilization evolve? And what causes winter mortality in trout? Sixty-five hundred feet up on the eastern slope of the Sierra Nevada, the museum has developed the Sagehen Creek Wildlife and Fisheries Station, where the trout swim free in the streams, and the observers are confined behind glass.

Since 1911, members of the museum staff have been active in wildlife conservation. In the course of their surveys, they continue to find many animals in danger of extinction, due to needless destruction of their habitats or public ignorance of their function in the ecology. The ruthless extermination of the great predators, such as falcons and eagles, wolves and mountain lions, has resulted in local overpopulations of their prey. Museum staff members regularly serve on conservation boards and advisory committees, conduct surveys and specific studies of game animals and threatened species, and help public education through the schools, movies, television, popular books, and magazine articles. Courses in wildlife ecology and management are given, and more and more museum graduates enter wildlife conservation as a profession.

Collections

Seth Benson, curator of mammals, is comparing the skulls of a killer whale and a porpoise. A. Starker Leopold, professor of zoology, inspects recent additions to the collection, brought back from Puerto Rico by Ned K. Johnson, curator of birds.

The Frances Simes Hastings Natural History Reservation

What has been the impact of man upon nature? How have his animals and his activities affected other life? In past ages his influence spread slowly. Now, every day, for human use, vast tracts of land are bulldozed clear. Whole habitats, whole ecologies are obliterated, and such wild plants and animals as survive must find other homes, adapt, or perish. Often scientists return to a place they have studied for years to find that, overnight, it has suffered irrevocable change. Areas undisturbed by human use, where the life cycles of plants and animals can be observed and recorded over perhaps as long as twenty years, are becoming rare.

Hastings Natural History Reservation: Observer, John Davis

The Frances Simes Hastings Natural History Reservation was set up in 1937 for just such observation. Cattle had been raised on the land for generations. Mr. and Mrs. Russell P. Hastings, seeking another use for these hills and valleys in the northern Santa Lucia Mountains, were so excited by discussions with the Museum of Vertebrate Zoology in Berkeley that they not only turned their ranch over to the museum, but contributed funds toward research and laboratories. The ranch was to return to nature. Grazing by cattle and sheep was stopped; fences were mended against strays, hunters, picnickers, dogs, and cats. The scientists who came to live in the little houses along the creek were to disturb plant life as little as possible by their comings and goings, and animal life not at all. No animal is ever killed. Animals caught for examination and identification are handled as briefly as possible and set free. Prey and predator, resident and migrant, are observed as they function in the ever-shifting balance of the ecology. Hours upon patient hours, the observers sit quietly on the ground with field glasses and notebooks, watching how various populations go on living around them and how particular animals react to the myriad situations of nature.

Holes and burrows now proliferate close to the little houses, and packrat nests rise close to headquarters. Fallen blue oaks, left as they fell, become homes to communities of lizards. The once-cropped grass now grows long, and almost extinct species are reviving. Only deer graze here: they hedge the chamise into low rounded mounds. Within a deer-proof fence, the chamise that sprang up after a recent wildfire is taller than a man and scarcely penetrable. Are deer perhaps not only a grace, but a necessity to the wildlands? And what roles are played by the mice, the birds, and the lizards?

At Hastings Reservation, the native populations in their natural relations are increasing. But the genotype, or what is believed to be the genotype—the original character of the region—is slow to return. Thirty years has not been long enough, so profound has been the impact of man.

Deep Canyon and the Coachella Valley

The Philip L. Boyd
Desert Research Center

Research on arid lands must begin in the desert itself. How does life in the desert adapt to such extremes as noon heat of 125°F in summer, and ice, frost, and even snow at 13°F on winter nights? How does it manage to lie dormant through long droughts, often for many years, and then after rain, suddenly awake to full vitality for a few brief hours or days? To what peculiar means has evolution formed certain species, and what can man learn therefrom?

Deep Canyon, the gift of Regent Philip L. Boyd to the University in 1959, is pure desert, uninfluenced by man. An awesome gash in the eastern flanks of the Santa Rosa Mountains, it plunges from the piñon and juniper on its rims down through several biotic zones to the flood-churned dry wash of the canyon floor four thousand feet below. Bighorn sheep haunt its crags, gazing forth motionless for hours; then suddenly, a whole band may flash down seemingly impassable precipices.

Cholla, Deep Canyon

Cycles of drought and rain succeed each other through long ages of slow climatic change. Southern California deserts have recently experienced the longest and most severe drought in four hundred years. Down on the alluvial fans and in the washes, desert willow, palo verde, cholla cactus, and even the stubborn creosote bush are dead or dying. Yet late one summer, one great storm, followed by a few autumn rains, suddenly brought forth in winter a burst of life and bloom surpassing the usual spring. But drought again returned, and once more the desert appeared to die. When—and if—the cycle of rain begins again, what will the transition be like? Which species of plant and animal will respond the earliest? What is the effect and function of the shattering, battering, eroding floods which hurl up banks and terraces? Some

plants, it appears, need abrasion by flood and stone to break their seed husks, as others need fire.

Most desert animals have become nocturnal, to avoid the intense heat of the day. By night, therefore, University zoologists tramp forth with flashlights and lanterns to waterholes and streams, to examine marked animals and observe their pursuits, conditions, and colonies. The animals, in turn, appear to regard the observers as merely large and harmless fauna with curious habits. By day, bucketing in jeeps up the washes and terraces and scrambling beyond the ends of trails, sometimes in almost unbearable heat and sometimes in one of the most delightful climates known, geologists and botanists go seeking and probing the strange phenomena of life in the desert.

The Ocean

The huge California coast appalled its first explorers.
A cold current pushed against them from the north.
Fogs bedevilled them: fogs at evening that swept over
their little ships like "a second sea," as one of
Drake's men wrote; morning fogs through which they
heard the cries of sea birds and the barking of "sea
wolves" before dimly discerning the ominous pallor of
surf around the offshore fangs of mountains that
vanished upward into mist. Sometimes the fog lifted,
and they looked from a diamond sea up steep,
desolate slopes to peaks against a deep blue sky.
Seldom did the fogs part to reveal a harbor, or even a
sheltering cove. On bright days, rare in summer, in the
afternoons the glitter of the westering sun on this
most immense of oceans increased to a blinding glare,
and then vanished softly, subtly, under the fogs
stealing in from the far horizon.

These same phenomena enthralled later explorers.
The icy sea, the fogs, and the bright sun foster a
wealth of marine life. With wonder and delight, men
watch grey whales pass spouting and sounding not far
from the surf. Each offshore rock seems to bear a
different colony: here sea lions bark; there elephant
seals bask enormous. Nearby, from rocks stained
white with guano, gulls rise shrieking above their
nests, while from steep perches below, cormorants
dive and swim underwater after fish. A little farther
out, flocks of shearwaters by the hundreds of
thousands come by, flying and swimming, on their
annual migration, circling the shores of the Pacific
from their home colonies in New Zealand. In the huge
kelp beds, sea otters play and float on their backs,
cradling their young. Fish and shellfish also abound:
the commercially valuable species—salmon, tuna, cod
and sole, crabs, clams, abalones, large prawns and
tiny shrimp—are only a few of the many species in
the Pacific.

Bodega Marine Laboratory

102

Bodega Marine Laboratory

"The biological diversity of the oceans—unequaled in any other environment on earth—provides the prime source material for many of the biological sciences," says Cadet Hand, professor of zoology at Berkeley and director of the new laboratory at Bodega. The laboratory fills an old need: scientists from the three northern campuses, Berkeley, Davis, and San Francisco, had no place to carry on marine research. They borrowed or rented whatever they could find by the sea shore—an old coast guard station, or a crab fisherman's gear shed. While prospecting for biologically rich sites, they discovered that around Bodega Head, only sixty-five miles from San Francisco, the beaches, cliffs, tide-flats, bays, and creeks were uniquely abundant in coastal and marine life. In 1961, the University purchased 326 acres of sand dunes, headlands, and coves across Bodega Head, and a year later, the National Science Foundation granted the $1,100,000 which made possible the construction of a multi-purpose laboratory beside Horseshoe Cove. There are two large laboratories for teaching, twenty-five smaller ones for research, large storage tanks, and several temperature chambers. The facility has space for sixty researchers and an equal number of undergraduates in summer courses.

The concrete laboratory is severely plain—its beauty is its aquariums. The fountain in the inner court is a series of seawater pools, one large enough for small leopard sharks. In the windows that look out on the court, there stand tall glass tanks in which huge sea anemones faintly wave their tentacles, barnacles pulse delicate filaments, abalones and snails move up the glass as they feed, and the eggcases of sea slugs, curled like a delicate ear, float close to the surface. The tanks in the seawater laboratories may contain anything except whales (too big): kelp and the colonies that inhabit it, fish, crustaceans, or tiny shrimplike forms, brilliant as jewels.

In many laboratories, divers' suits and boots hang from the ceiling. The surf and rocks off Bodega are rough and dangerous for that awkward animal, a diver in full rig, so plastic whaleboats carry him out to where he can go down into the ocean, as free as a fish. Inshore, and offshore for a thousand feet, the station is a biological refuge and a biologist's delight.

Sea Anemones, Mendocino Coast

On land, the first characteristic of any animal is movement.
Running, leaping, flying, slithering, scuttling, it seeks its food
or flees from its enemies. But in the sea, many animals have no
need to move anything more than the filaments or tentacles near
their mouths. Rooted, like these sea anemones, they wait while
the sea, with its rich bounty, floats food toward them.

Scripps Institution of Oceanography

The Scripps Pier

Built in 1915, the long pier is now used chiefly by small craft and scuba divers, though meteorological and other observations continue to be recorded in the station at its outer end, and seawater conversion studies are conducted at its base on the shore. Its pumps still supply seawater to the aquariums in the museum and the laboratories.

In 1892, William E. Ritter, professor of zoology at Berkeley, began making a survey of Pacific marine animals. Every summer for a decade, he set up a coastal field station in a different locality. In 1903, Ritter decided on La Jolla as the ideal permanent base, and there continued his research with the support of the San Diego Marine Biological Association. The newspaper publisher E. W. Scripps and his half sister Ellen gave generously toward the development of the facility and its scientific programs. The Regents accepted the facility as the Scripps Institution for Biological Research in 1912, but in 1925, decided to change its name to the Scripps Institution of Oceanography. By this time, the interests of its scientists had broadened to include every aspect of the study of oceans. In addition to biologists, the faculty of the institution now included geologists, geographers, physicists, chemists, meteorologists, and even astronomers. Already Scripps ranked with Monaco, Naples, and Wood's Hole as one of the world's great oceanographic institutions.

Oceanography proved of vital importance during World War II, and afterwards, with federal and foundation grants and in close collaboration with the United States Navy, Scripps was precipitated into an enormously expanded program. Its faculty doubled; its staff, especially in the higher academic ratings, increased eight-fold; facilities, such as the carbon-14 and the tritium laboratories and new docks in the harbor of San Diego, were added. Its fleet grew from one schooner, in 1907, to ten research ships, including the *Alpha Helix,* a sea-going laboratory buttressed against arctic ice and air-conditioned for the tropics, and the revolutionary *FLIP* (Floating Instrument Platform), which is towed horizontally, and, when flipped, stands vertically three hundred feet deep in the sea, stable as a fence post in the quiet depths not even a hurricane or a typhoon can disturb.

Scripps ships have sailed on voyages of thousands of miles in all the oceans, mapping the ocean floor, discovering undersea mountains and canyons, measuring the temperatures of currents and heat-flow patterns, collecting specimens from every depth, and

Physiologist, Scripps Institution of Oceanography

Per F. Scholander, professor of physiology and director of the Physiological Research Laboratory at Scripps, in the crow's nest of the *Alpha Helix*. Scholander is interested in marine neurobiology and especially in porpoises. In 1966, he led the Billabong, or Great Barrier Reef Expedition, to Australia on the first cruise of the *Alpha Helix*.

charting the migrations and life cycles of fish, birds, mammals, crustaceans, and all the multitudinous forms of life in the sea. Ingenious minds, skilled technicians in the workshops, and a crew of roustabouts are needed to devise and employ the drills, thermometers, and dragnets which seem so slight compared to the power of the sea.

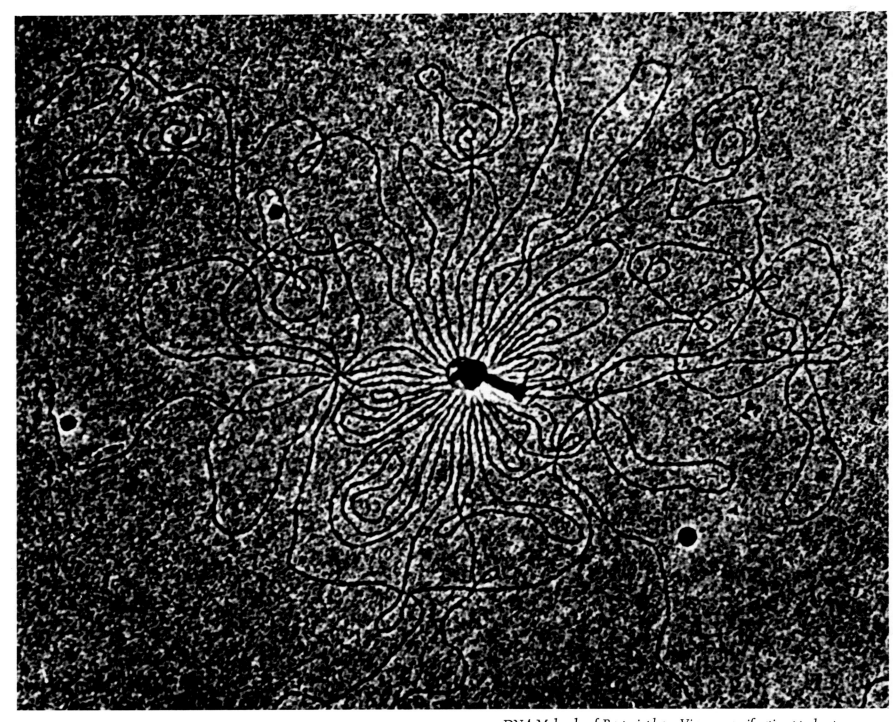

DNA Molecule of Bacteriophage Virus, magnification × about 112,000
Virus Laboratory Photograph

Virus Laboratory, Berkeley

Of the new sciences born in the last two decades, none has more tremendous implications than molecular genetics. The geneticists who, around 1900, began carrying further the discoveries of Mendel, proved several important theses: that the traits of organisms are indeed heritable, that their chromosomes contain the genetic message that passes relatively intact from parent to child, and that mutations can cause variations in the otherwise smooth and endless passage of hereditary material. It was even possible to make genetic maps and discover what portions of the chromosomes were responsible for a variety of hereditary traits. But the key was missing: what factor in the chromosomes actually constitutes the genetic message, the information passed from one generation to the next?

In the 1940's, it was finally established that viruses, as well as cells, contain hereditary material, that they can breed true and are subject to mutations. Since viruses are the simplest form of self-reproducing objects, though capable of remaking their kind only within a living cell, and since many of them contain only two chemicals, proteins and nucleic acids, it shortly became apparent that the hereditary material of life *must* be nucleic acid. Detailed investigations of viruses pointed to further examination of nucleic acids, both DNA and RNA. In 1953, Crick and Watson, in Cambridge, postulated the now accepted structure of DNA: a two-stranded helix, either of whose strands can separate and preside over the replication of its fellow. The older concept of the gene became irrelevant, since it was now clear that the sequence of nucleotides, the components of DNA, constitute the genetic message. When these sequences pass undisturbed to progeny, whether cells or viruses, the new organisms are much like the old; when breaks and substitutions occur, the progeny may suffer drastic change: a mutation has taken place. The study of the molecular structure of nucleic acids and the manner in which this structure controls the function of the cell or virus constitutes the science of modern genetics.

Viruses, formerly investigated only because they are agents of dread diseases, have made it possible for molecular biologists to explore genetics at a level of detail and of comprehension undreamed of by Mendel and his early followers.

Wendell M. Stanley, a biochemist, had already been awarded the Nobel Prize for isolating and characterizing a virus in pure form when he came to Berkeley in 1948 to found a new research organization, the Virus Laboratory, first of its kind on a university campus. Stanley soon gathered about him an extraordinarily able group of scientists, many originally trained in other disciplines. The laboratory has become one of the foremost virus research centers in the world, and the only one in which work on all kinds of viruses is in progress. Its many achievements include the production of pure polio virus and its crystallization for the first time, and the discovery that the pure nucleic acid of a virus was competent to infect cells and cause the formation of new viruses. The laboratory's approach throughout has been that of the molecular

biologist: to use viruses in attempting to unravel the tangled skein of life, as probes to discover how cells transfer their genetic message and use their genetic material to regulate their function. A new academic department of molecular biology, formed in 1964, now works in close cooperation with the Virus Laboratory; running throughout the joint operation is the important quest for understanding the role of molecular genetics in the living process and its replication.

Virus Laboratory, Berkeley

Donald A. Glaser, professor of physics and molecular biology, received the 1960 Nobel Prize in physics "for the invention of the bubble chamber." After which, to use his own phrase, he "went back to school," and entered the new field of molecular biology, to the amazement of his fellow Laureates. At present, he regards his design for producing and handling thousands of mutations of viruses within a twenty-four-hour period as "just engineering."

Geology

Geology, both as a pure and as an applied science, has played a dynamic, even a crucial, role in California. Gold in the creeks and veins of the Mother Lode, silver in the Comstock Lode just over the border in Nevada, borax hauled by twenty-mule teams from Death Valley, oil wells gushing up in Los Angeles back yards—these are a few of the bonanzas that have attracted millions of people to California. Yet of the millions who came to exploit, there are thousands who have remained to love this tremendous country and its contrasts.

Geology Field Trip, Riverside

The Riverside campus is surrounded by a wide variety of geological phenomena of intense interest both to scientists and practicing professional geologists. Here Gordon P. Eaton, associate professor of geology and chairman of the department at Riverside, and Frank W. Dickson, professor of geology and geophysics, lead a group of graduates into Joshua Tree National Monument. The towering rock forms are actually the granite roots of an ancient mountain range.

The University's concern with geology in both its branches began when it hired among its first professors two internationally known scientists, the brothers LeConte. John, a physicist, taught industrial mechanics, and served among the early presidents of the University. Joseph taught geology, botany, and natural history. The Sierra Nevada became his consuming delight; mountain structure and earthquakes obsessed him, as they have countless of his successors.

Another scientist, Samuel H. Christy, became head of the College of Mining in 1885, and laid out the laboratories for one of the first adequately equipped mining schools in the world. Phoebe Apperson Hearst had John Galen Howard design a building with multiple chimneys—"a shell for the future to fill in"— where mining students could set up forges, make assays, and experiment with drills. The College of Mining became world-renowned; students came to it from as far away as Peru and South Africa. While petroleum, tungsten, copper, molybdenum, rare earths, and even gold are still mined in California, the interests of students have changed. Their excitement now focuses on geological and geophysical science and engineering, metallurgy, ceramics, and the highest theoretical training in electromagnetics and thermo-dynamics, which are the best preparation for practical technology as well as the educated guessing necessary to aerospace engineering.

In geology, as in all science, practice and theory converge, bringing with them a wide variety of scientists from other disciplines. Today at the University, undergraduates are given the basic outlines of the history and evolution of the earth as quickly as possible, and are then encouraged to concentrate on their special interest. Geology is still full of unexplored areas. Each new discovery, such as the use of radioisotopes in dating, produces the same delight and curiosity felt by Joseph LeConte, John Muir, Josiah Whitney, William Brewer, and the many others whose names remain upon the peaks and trails they explored.

Geology and biology have already led men down into the deep sea and out into space. The gold prospector with pickaxe and burro gave way to the uranium prospector with a jeep and a Geiger counter; now even the prospector in a jet plane with radar and infrared photography, or in a bathysphere thousands of feet down in the ocean, is being replaced by artificial satellites, manned or unmanned, ranging among the planets and recording information that may answer some of our questions about the earth.

White Mountain High Altitude Research Station

White Mountain Peak stands 14,250 feet above sea level, the third highest mountain in California. Only its neighbors, Mount Williamson and Mount Whitney, surpass it. White Mountain looks out upon magnificence: eastward, down through labyrinths of granite canyons and valleys jewelled with lakes and meadows to the vast and desolate Nevada desert; westward, down steep slopes plunging to the sagebrush-dotted Owens Valley two miles below, and across to the huge fault scarp of the Sierra Nevada, whose domes and spires, visible here for more than three hundred miles, often emerge from swirling storms to shine bright with snow.

In the midst of such grandeur, no one had paid much attention to the White Mountain Range itself—there were but a few ranchers riding through, an occasional group of mountaineers, and periodic patrols by the United States Forest Service—until 1948, when the United States Navy set up a small station at Crooked Creek, at an elevation of 10,000 feet, for research connected with guided missiles. One of the station's early visitors was Nello Pace, a dynamic young physiologist from Berkeley who had done distinguished wartime research for the Navy and who had commanded the radiological survey after the atomic bombing of Hiroshima and Nagasaki. For Pace, to investigate the miraculous mechanisms by which life adapts itself to extremes is the greatest challenge science offers today, and he will go anywhere to find out more about it. He fell in love with White Mountain at first sight, and exploration only confirmed his ardor. The peak rises through every climatic and biotic zone from desert to alpine—with Death Valley, 290 feet below sea level, only 80 miles away.

Haldane Gas Analysis Apparatus and White Mountain Peak

The broad back of the range, with 120 square miles above 10,000 feet, constituted the next best thing to a platform in space. For biologists, the bighorn sheep in the crags to the north and the ancient bristlecone pines on the lunar slopes around 11,000 feet—later found to be the oldest living things yet discovered—offered a rich field of research. Within a hundred-mile radius, geologists could study a range of phenomena as remarkable as any on earth. Astronomers, at this height and clarity, could discover and measure much that eluded them in lower and more polluted atmospheres.

In 1950, by agreement with the Navy and the Forest Service, responsibility for research at White Mountain was transferred to the University. With funds and material from the Navy, grants from the Rockefeller Foundation, the National Institutes of Health, the National Science Foundation, and, later, the National Aeronautics and Space Administration (NASA), Pace set out to build the highest permanent research facility in North America and one of the highest anywhere. Graduate students volunteered to help build the stations: one, a stone hut on the summit; another, containing the major research laboratories, animal pens and cages, and living quarters, on Mount Barcroft, at 12,500 feet; and third, an enlarged facility at Crooked Creek. They fought the energy-sapping altitudes and the high winds; they coaxed huge equipment up the winding and bone-shattering rocky roads; they developed enormous ingenuity in adapting Navy surplus material; and they toiled to roof in and make snug whatever they were working on before the relentless snows descended.

Today, White Mountain High Altitude Research Station functions the year round. Often its three stations are in or above the clouds. Sometimes they are buried in snow, at temperatures as low as —32°F, when only the "weasels" can get around. A helicopter, thanks to NASA, regularly transports men, animals, and materials to and from the mountain. The quality and the diversity of the work done here by scientists from many disciplines, universities, and nations already place White Mountain among the foremost research stations in the world.

Nello Pace and Astromonkey

Nello Pace, professor of physiology-anatomy at Berkeley, chairman of the department and director of the White Mountain High Altitude Research Station, leads a number of simultaneous scientific lives. He commutes regularly to White Mountain, usually by helicopter, where he has several research projects to attend to as well as his administrative duties. He teaches a full schedule at the Berkeley campus, and his classic answer to great questions—"Gee whiz, let's go there and find out!"—continues to fire his students and colleagues with such enthusiasm that they follow him, literally, to the ends of the earth. He led a joint United States Army-Navy team to study combat stress in Korea, served as chief scientist and deputy leader on the 1954 Himalayan Expedition to Makalu, and directed the 1957–58 International Physiological Expedition to the Antarctic. Now he would love to be among the first men to set foot on the moon or Mars! But that adventure, the greatest man will have ever attempted, will be for his sons in spirit. Meanwhile, he is doing everything he can think of to investigate space flight.

In the basement of the old fraternity house he uses for a laboratory in Berkeley, Pace has engineered devices that simulate every condition of space flight, including acceleration up to twenty G's. Here he works with a charming troupe of pale gray, pigtailed monkeys who have been instrumented so that every physiological reaction to acceleration, weightlessness, confinement, radiation, and other hazards can be recorded. He is very proud of his monkeys. Their cages bear labels such as, "Belisarius. Completed 93 days confinement." One has actually completed two hundred days of simulated space flight, and from among them, some will be chosen to go on a real journey to a biosatellite, orbiting twenty-two thousand miles above the earth for long periods before they are brought down again, hopefully alive and well.

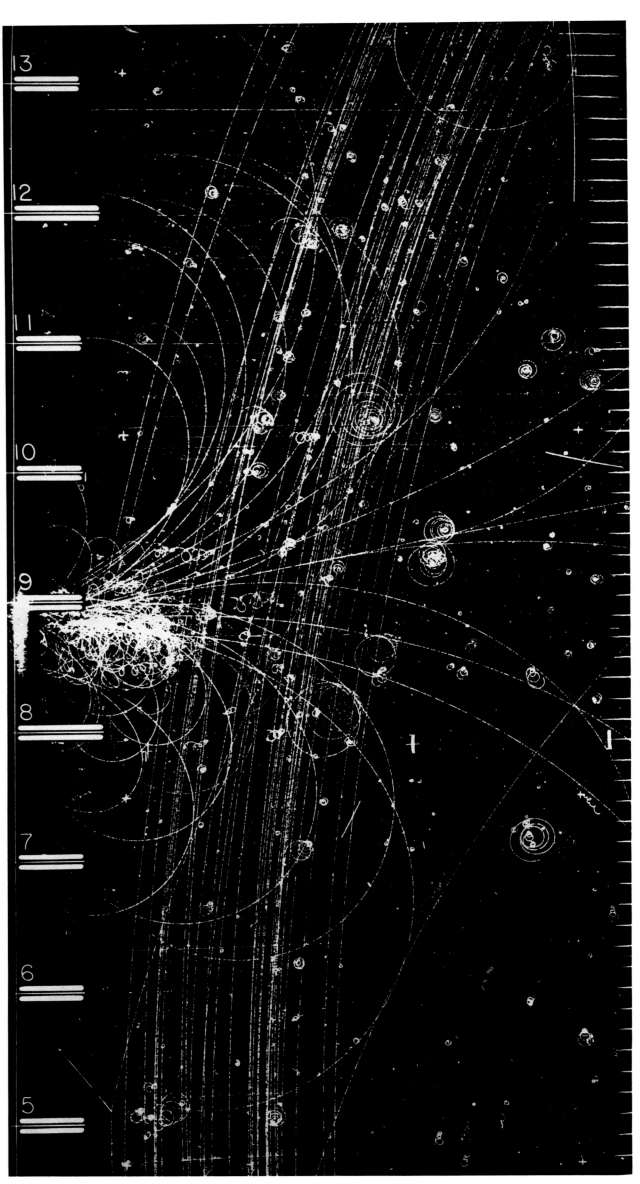

Bubble Chamber Event

In a storm of ions, a cosmic ray generated in outer space intrudes on the flight of particles generated in the Bevatron, which are themselves man-made cosmic rays.

Immensely powerful cosmic rays bombard this planet constantly. Colliding with particles in the upper atmosphere, they give rise to showers of secondary particles which continually fall in a gentle, invisible rain upon the earth, some penetrating even through lead to mines far below the earth's surface.

In the 1930's, scientists perceived that this cosmic rain consisted of the basic particles from which all matter is formed. An early instrument for visualizing and studying cosmic rays was the Wilson cloud chamber, in which particles passing through water vapor left gossamer tracks that could be photographed. But in nature, even on high mountain peaks, or at altitudes once accessible only to balloons, few nuclear events revealing the creation of new elementary particles are commonly recorded.

Then, in the late 1940's, the cyclotrons invented by Ernest Lawrence at Berkeley reached a magnitude by which, for the first time, cosmic rays could be generated in the laboratory, eventually in profuse beams greatly increasing the incidence of such nuclear events, so that man at last could study them at will.

More sensitive detectors were needed. Nobel Laureate Donald Glaser invented the bubble chamber, and Luis Alvarez and his colleagues at Berkeley developed it into the present seventy-two-inch chamber, using liquid hydrogen or deuterium, with a tri-stereo photography system and instruments to measure, analyze, and compute. Prototype of many others built around the world, the bubble chamber, harnessed with that great Berkeley descendant of the cyclotron, the massive Bevatron, has made possible the discovery of fundamental particles of matter whose very existence was not suspected before.
Lawrence Radiation Laboratory photograph

THE NUCLEAR SCIENCES

Of what is the universe composed: of particles discrete, like sand—the *atom,* the indivisible, of the Greeks? or of energy in waves, like the sea? What forms and forces order this primordial matter into the marvelous phenomena perceivable by man—sun, stars, oceans, mountains, clouds, light, leaves, and life, including this pulsing, breathing, thinking form man now inhabits—and the still more marvellous phenomena extending infinitely beyond the narrow range of his earthbound senses?

Telescopes, microscopes, and many other subtle instruments, electricity, magnetism, thermodynamics, and many other discoveries of unknown forces had extended man's knowledge by the end of the nineteenth century. Nevertheless, he still conceived the atom as indivisible, when a totally unforeseen means of inquiry was revealed through the discovery of radioactivity. The excitement was international, linking together in one of the most astounding intellectual chain reactions in the history of science the genius of Becquerel, Marie Curie, Lord Rutherford, Max Planck, Albert Einstein, Niels Bohr, and many others. In the United States, the excitement and the genius came to focus at Berkeley.

Gilbert Lewis and the College of Chemistry, Berkeley

Gilbert Newton Lewis, a physical chemist, came, in 1912, from the Massachusetts Institute of Technology to serve as dean of the College of Chemistry at Berkeley and to build up its graduate and research programs. Lewis was already known for his work in thermodynamics and his interest in radioactivity and the atom, which he had acquired during his studies at Leipzig and Goettingen. Young chemists flocked to him from all over America. Richard C. Tolman, Joel H. Hildebrand, and G. Ernest Gibson were among the first to join the faculty; soon their ranks were augmented by their former graduate students, such as Wendell Latimer, and W. F. Giauque, who had intended to be an engineer but became so fascinated by chemical thermodynamics, magnetism, and low temperature research that he stayed in Berkeley, eventually to receive the Nobel Prize. Another graduate student, however, who was to be the first of the group to achieve that honor, rushed off before taking his doctorate in person: Harold C. Urey had received a fellowship enabling him to study in Copenhagen under Niels Bohr.

Bohr, in 1913, from his work with Rutherford, had evolved the concept that the atom in structure is similar to the solar system, the heavy nucleus like the sun in the system's center, with the light electrons traveling in planetary orbits about it. With the broader and more sophisticated understanding which soon followed, Lewis could, in 1916, elucidate to his students the difference between nuclear physics and nuclear chemistry: physics concerned the heavy nucleus, chemistry the planetary electrons and the chemical bonds between them. Lewis also was among the first to see clearly that the energy source of the actual sun could only be atomic energy.

To his students, Lewis was a constant inspiration. One of them, Nobel Laureate Willard Libby, considers, "No great scientist has ever been so poorly celebrated as this colossus of the modern world." Another, Melvin Calvin, also a Laureate, said, "He was the greatest scientist I have ever known. He had complete freedom of imagination . . . unsurpassed accuracy of intuition, governed by a careful consideration for experimental results. He was not afraid to undertake anything, and he encouraged me to do the same."

Ernest Lawrence and the Radiation Laboratory

In the physics department, a similar excitement was rising. A young associate professor, Ernest O. Lawrence, already the originator of new devices and methods for studying ionization, had for some time been contemplating the problem of accelerating ions. Rutherford, in 1919, while bombarding nitrogen atoms with the alpha particles naturally emitted from radium, achieved what the alchemists could not: the transmutation of one element into another. Some, a very few, of the nitrogen atoms became oxygen. To carry the transmutations further, more powerful accelerators were needed. Cockcroft and Walton designed one, and so did Van de Graff. Still, the beams they generated could not penetrate the nuclei of the heavy elements. In 1929, Lawrence, glancing over a sketch in a German magazine, suddenly conceived and formulated, within minutes, the principle of the cyclotron. This he demonstrated before the National Academy of Sciences in 1930. Between the simple, brilliant concept and its realization in a fully operating machine lay formidable engineering

problems never encountered before. With a daring, an inventiveness, and a persistence rare even in science, Lawrence tackled them. Down in the basement of old LeConte Hall, he produced a 4.5-inch instrument of brass and wax in which, on January 3, 1931, an energy of 80,000 electron volts was achieved with protons. Before the year was out, with an 11-inch cyclotron, the million-electron-volt mark (MeV) was exceeded for the first time in history. With this, Lawrence also achieved the first artificial disintegration of the nucleus in the United States.

Cyclotron followed cyclotron as Lawrence reached for new energy ranges. Edwin M. McMillan, one of Lawrence's earliest associates, remembers those days: "We did practically everything ourselves. We had no professional engineers, so we had to design our own apparatus; we made sketches for the shop, and did much of our machine work; we took all our own data, did all our calculations, and wrote all of our own papers."

After Harold Urey discovered deuterium in nature in 1932, Lewis proceeded to isolate the "heavy water" himself, gave one drop to a laboratory mouse, who, it it is said, merely cried for more, and the other to Lawrence, who also cried for more. Bombardment by deuterons proved more prolific of results than any previous beam. In 1934, the Joliot-Curies in Paris cabled to Lawrence their discovery of artificial radioactivity; Lawrence, that same night, found it in his own laboratory, due to a recent bombardment with deuterons. Within a few hours, he and his colleagues discovered several new radioisotopes.

In the years that followed, scores of new radioisotopes were discovered at Berkeley. Soon after a medical specialist yearned aloud for an isotope for studying iron in the body, iron-59 was produced, and it has revolutionized knowledge of blood metabolism and disease. A thyroid researcher needed a corresponding tool, and iodine-131 was created. On the imposing list of useful isotopes created at Berkeley are hydrogen-3 (tritium), helium-3, and carbon-14.

Lawrence encouraged such interdisciplinary collaboration. He urged chemists and physicists to work with biologists and physicians, and, because of the need for new instrumentation, urged that each group engaged in solving a particular problem should include a professional engineer. He himself initiated at the University's Medical Center the first million-volt x-ray machine. It was at the Center that the first experiment using a radioactive tracer in humans was performed; with sodium-24 from the cyclotron and a counter, it was learned that the speed of metabolism was much greater than had been assumed. Characteristically, when the cyclotron began producing radioisotopes in some quantity, Lawrence shipped part of the supply of radiophosphorus to the great Hungarian, deHevesy, who had pioneered in tracer studies using the natural isotopes of lead.

In 1936, the scale and complexity of the research and engineering centering around Lawrence and the cyclotron were such that the Regents created the Radiation Laboratory as a separate administrative unit. The prototype of the big laboratory was now established.

In 1939, Lawrence was awarded the Nobel Prize for "the invention and development of the cyclotron, and or the results thereby attained, especially with regard to artificial radioelements."

"His cyclotron is to nuclear science what Galileo's telescope was to astronomy. . . . He had the vision to glimpse the limitless nature of the horizon and the generosity to make room for others. His personal credo was, 'There is enough research for all of us to do.' He interceded, with his rare persuasiveness, to create new facilities for worthy projects. He rejoiced as jubilantly in the success of others as in his own. As a result, the careers of many scientists, my own included, are founded on his large contribution and his generous nature. Indeed, so great was the opportunity he created that he was influential in the training of a significant portion of the present corps of nuclear scientists."

GLENN T. SEABORG

The Transuranium Elements

There was great need in 1939 not only for the young scientists Lawrence had trained, but for his own remarkable qualities as scientist and statesman. For some years, theorists had predicted that uranium, element 92 in the periodic table, the last and heaviest of the natural elements, could be transmuted into element 93—one of those so short-lived and so unstable that soon after the nuclear fires that created all elements died from the solar system, they decayed into the stable elements we know, and no longer exist except when synthesized by man. Fermi believed he had synthesized element 93; others claimed it too, but the majority of their peers and colleagues could not confirm their findings. In the course of such tests, Otto Hahn in Germany discovered nuclear fission.

No one expected so violent a rearrangement of matter. With World War II beginning to darken whole continents, the implications were ominous: the atom bomb was clearly discernable. On which side achieved this terrible weapon first might hang the future of the world. A committee of scientists, several of them refugees, persuaded President Roosevelt to initiate the investigation of the potentials of nuclear fission for military purposes.

McMillan, in Berkeley, in trying to ascertain how far the products of fission traveled, found a puzzling phenomenon he suspected might be the elusive element 93. With P. H. Abelson, in the summer of 1940, he proved it, and called it neptunium, because the planet Neptune lies beyond Uranus. He was working on element 94 when he was called away to direct radar research at Massachusetts Institute of Technology. Glenn Seaborg and others of his colleagues continued the experiments, and, in 1941, synthesized plutonium, and its isotope Pu^{239}, the nuclear fuel, more fissionable than uranium.

The rest is history: Lawrence's persistence, energy, and ideas catalyzed the project. An unequaled constellation of scientists, including refugees, worked in various places throughout the United States—at Berkeley, at the University of Chicago, at Oak Ridge, Tennessee, and finally, when in 1943 the United States asked the University of California to organize and administer the world's first nuclear weapons plant, at Los Alamos, New Mexico. The weapon was developed in time to be important in ending the war in the Pacific.

Even before the end of the war, the great march of the transuranic elements began again, with a team of Berkeley scientists headed by A. Ghiorso and Glenn Seaborg in Chicago discovering 95, Americium, and 96, Curium, at the University of Chicago. Two more elements were discovered back in Berkeley, and another two, together with the Argonne and Los Alamos Laboratories, from materials created during the first hydrogen bomb explosion at Eniwetok in 1952. Eventually the periodic table was extended to element 103, named Lawrencium.

Lawrence Radiation Laboratory, Berkeley

Edwin M. McMillan, professor of physics and director of the Lawrence Radiation Laboratory, at the console of the Bevatron. McMillan and Glenn T. Seaborg, professor of chemistry and now chairman, Atomic Energy Commission, shared the Nobel Prize in 1951 "for their discoveries in the chemistry of the transuranic elements." McMillan also shared the Atoms for Peace Award in 1963 with V. Veksler, a Russian physicist, for their independent discovery of the theory of phase stability which made possible such multi-billion-electron-volt accelerators as the Bevatron.

In Berkeley, in 1948, a new era in particle physics began when the 184-inch cyclotron, into which McMillan's theory of phase stability had been successfully incorporated, produced for the first time mesons, particles previously produced only by cosmic rays. Recorded on photographic plates placed near the target, the mesons opened up inquiry into the whole subatomic universe. Lawrence commented that since the cyclotron had barely enough power to produce mesons, mightier atom smashers were needed. With the Bevatron, 6.2 billion electron volts became available in 1954, and in 1955, Emilio Segrè, who had previously synthesized two elements missing from the periodic table, and Owen Chamberlain discovered the anti-proton and the strange mirror world of anti-matter. For this discovery, Chamberlain and Segrè received the Nobel Prize in 1959.

In 1952, the Atomic Energy Commission asked Lawrence to set up a second nuclear weapons laboratory, at the old United States Naval Air Station at Livermore, California. Here, applied research in nuclear and thermonuclear power, led by Herbert York and Edward Teller, developed both weapons and new uses of these powers for peace. Lawrence, whose conviction that strength is the only shield for free institutions was accompanied by the hope that peace could be made permanent, died in 1958. The Regents rechristened the now vast laboratory, with its many branches on its triple sites, in his honor.

The search into the subatomic particles continues. About a third of the eighty now known have been discovered at Berkeley. They have revolutionized man's concept of matter, but they have not yet answered his question: What are the basic building blocks of the universe? There may be three, which have been dubbed "the quarks," or there may be one, endlessly developing and diversifying, combining, decaying, and renewing, for which time is a merely local phenomenon.

Lawrence Radiation Laboratory, Berkeley

The Bevatron, in which an energy of 6.2 billion electron volts (BeV) is reached in two seconds, and a beam of 1,000 billion particles per pulse is delivered at 99.13 percent of the speed of light at the target.

Donner Laboratory of Medical Physics and Biophysics, Berkeley

Dr. John H. Lawrence was already working, at Yale, on the effects of radiation and means to prevent or offset them when he came to visit his brother Ernest in Berkeley in the summer of 1935. With the twenty-seven-inch cyclotron, radioactive substances previously unknown to man were being derived from such common elements as phosphorus and iron. Dr. Lawrence recalls: "Watching all the young men working around the cyclotron bombarding new targets and measuring the radiations with Geiger counters and Wilson cloud chambers, I was soon infected with the excitement of the early experiments and spent the remainder of the summer here. Very little was known of the biological effects of the neutron rays produced by the cyclotron, and this seemed an important place to start work."

With Paul Aebersold, then a graduate student, and later head of the Isotopes Division of the Atomic Energy Commission, Dr. Lawrence collected mice, a microscope, blood-counting pipettes, and an ionization chamber, and, as one part of the study, began comparing the effects of neutrons with those of x-rays. Loading their Model A Ford with mice, they would cross the Bay on the ferry to get the x-ray exposures at the University's Medical School. In their first experiment with the cyclotron, in Berkeley, they placed a rat in a metal cylinder in the neutron beam for two minutes—an arbitrary time, since no one knew what to expect. When they took it out, the rat was dead. The laboratory, appalled, began, with John Lawrence's help, to set up measures for protection against radiation which laid the foundations for safety in the Atomic Age. When, a few days later, histological sections proved that the rat had actually died of suffocation—they had forgotten to turn on the air inlet—Dr. Lawrence said little about it. Remembering what happened to the early workers with x-rays and radium, he continued his search into the effects of radiation. By the end of the summer, he and Aebersold had proven that neutron rays were five times as destructive to living tissue as x-rays, and might be even more effective than x-rays in treating cancer, tumors, and other growths.

Because of their radioactivity, the new artificial isotopes the cyclotron was producing could be traced through the intricate life-systems of plants and animals—a method of exploring the hitherto unknown and inaccessible as revolutionary as the microscope, and today considered as essential. Many isotopes of the common elements found in living things have very short lives—seconds, minutes, hours—while others have half-lives of months or years. The cyclotron at Berkeley being at that time the sole producer of isotopes in the world, Dr. Lawrence, urged by the great brain surgeon Harvey Cushing to continue his researches into the tremendous potentials of isotopes, left Yale and came to Berkeley. In his initial studies, he learned much about the metabolism of common elements in the body. Therapeutic effects of isotopes soon appeared, especially in diseases of the blood and bone marrow; success in treating animals having leukemia led Dr. Lawrence, on Christmas Eve, 1937, to administer a radioisotope to a human being in treatment for the first time. It proved beneficial; thousands with chronic leukemia have since been helped by it. The first control of disease through radiotherapy was achieved in 1938, when three patients suffering from polycthemia vera, a life-shortening disease of the blood, recovered after small doses of radiophosphorus. More than five hundred patients have been thus treated over the last twenty years; they are symptom-free and have a near-normal life expectancy.

When the sixty-inch cyclotron began operating in 1939, a vastly expanded range and quantity of isotopes became available. The Lawrences began shipping them free to scientists, hospitals, and laboratories around the world.

The physicians, physicists, chemists, and biologists who came to work with John Lawrence in the old Radiation Laboratory rapidly established their group as the world's first center for research and teaching in the uses of atomic energy in biology and medicine. In 1941, funds for a separate laboratory building were donated by William H. Donner, president of the

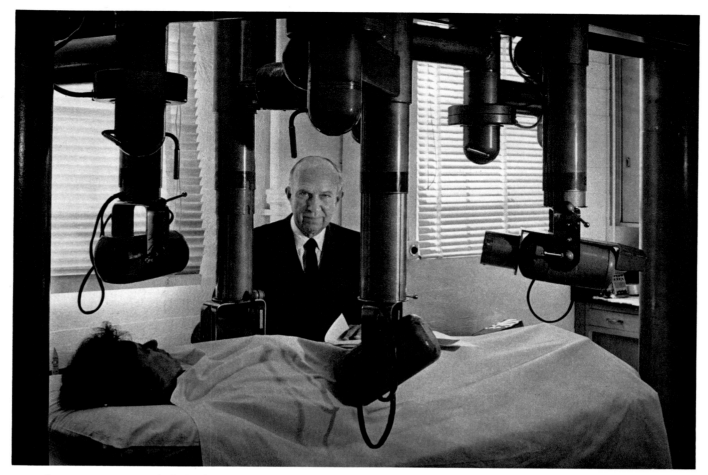

Dr. John H. Lawrence, with the multiple-port in vivo counter
One of the main instruments and techniques devised at Donner Laboratory for the use of radioisotopes in medical investigation and diagnosis.

Donner Foundation, in memory of his son who died of cancer.

The new laboratory was scarcely completed when it was taken over in part by the Manhattan Project. High-altitude stress and its effects in those days of unpressurized airplane cabins, development of oxygen equipment and of parachutes that broke free fall by opening through increasing air pressure, study of decompression sickness (the bends), air-sea rescue techniques, and the construction of the first low-pressure chamber were some of Donner Laboratory's wartime contributions.

High-altitude studies continue. In the 1950's, Dr. Lawrence led expeditions into the Andes to study native populations living at 14,900 to 17,000 feet above sea level. Dr. William Siri, in anticipation of the 1963 American climb of Mount Everest, spent four days in the low-pressure chamber trying out on himself conditions expected in the Himalayas.

The broad spectrum of research now pursued at the laboratory includes mutation, genetic control, development, and aging; arteriosclerosis and heart disease; and the mechanisms of learning and memory. The research with heavy particles begun by Dr. Lawrence in 1935 has developed, with the collaboration of Dr. Cornelius A. Tobias and others, into the use of beams from cyclotrons and linear accelerators as "atomic knife" surgery on brain tumors, breast cancer, and such pituitary and endocrine-related diseases as Cushing's and Parkinson's diseases. Dr. Tobias, a pioneer in the biology of heavy particles, has been investigating for the National Aeronautics and Space Administration the probable effects on space explorers of the Van Allen belt, solar flares, and the bombardment of heavy ions in outer space, and how to insulate space vehicles against them. Dr. Tobias is also head of the Division of Medical Physics, through which undergraduate, graduate, and post-doctoral students have been trained to carry on radiation research and therapy in most of the countries of the world. Virtually every medical center now uses atomic medical techniques.

The magnetic coil of ALICE, and Charles C. Damm, physicist,
in charge of the ALICE group, Livermore.

Project Sherwood, Lawrence Radiation Laboratory, Livermore

Thermonuclear power is the energy source of all stars, except possibly the quasars. For billions of years, at temperatures of many million degrees centigrade, hydrogen nuclei have been fusing to form helium nuclei. Through this cycle, vast amounts of radiant energy emitted by the stars—in the form of heat, visible light, and streams of charged particles—are given forth. At stellar temperatures, all matter becomes the ionized gas called plasma, sometimes called "the fourth state of matter." The three states of matter familiar to us on earth—solid, liquid, and gas —are actually almost unique in the universe. Ninety-nine per cent of all matter, so astrophysicists assure us, is in plasma form.

To achieve controlled thermonuclear energy on earth, one must create a hot plasma composed of thermo-nuclear power and then learn to hold and control it. Actually, both the principles of thermonuclear fusion and the strange and puzzling behavior of plasmas were encountered in the laboratory before nuclear fission. But nuclear fission, involving a chain reaction at ordinary temperatures and using heavy elements high in the periodic table, proved simpler to create and control. Fission, in the form of the atom bomb, was used to ignite the hydrogen bomb, which is thermonuclear fusion uncontrolled.

All present sources of energy used by man are subject to grave objections. The use of oil and coal, whether because of depletion, or because of pollution of the atmosphere, will doubtless soon be curtailed. Nuclear reactors, though potential producers of enormous amounts of power from a relatively abundant source—uranium and thorium, pose the problem of disposing of highly dangerous radioactive wastes and ashes, with half-lives of thousands of years. But, if physicists learn how to control and contain thermonuclear fusion, man will have unlimited and non-polluting energy from a virtually inexhaustible source, the heavy hydrogen of the oceans—the ultimate energy resource for fusion.

At Los Alamos, around the end of World War II, Enrico Fermi, Edward Teller, James Tuck, and others considered the possibility of attaining fusion power through confining hot plasma within some kind of magnetic field. However, no extensive experiments were carried out in the United States until 1951, when the United States Atomic Energy Commission initiated, under the code name Project Sherwood, a long-range program of research aimed at achieving fusion power. At Livermore, Berkeley, Los Alamos, Princeton University, Oak Ridge, and elsewhere, these experiments remained secret until the United States Atoms for Peace Conference at Geneva in 1958. Since then, scientists from Russia, the United Kingdom, France, Italy, Japan, and other nations freely and frequently exchange theories and discoveries on what is perhaps the most difficult and challenging technical problem man has ever set himself to solve: to attain and control on earth the power of the stars. In the stars and in the sun, the hot gases from fusion are confined within the gravitational forces of immense masses isolated in empty space. On earth, we must find other means of control and isolation. It is hoped that magnetic fields will provide the answer.

Edward Teller once compared attempting to confine plasma in a magnetic field to trying to weave out of rubber bands a basket to hold lukewarm jello. Man-made satellites, however, have confirmed that this phenomenon (of magnetic confinement) exists in nature: the Van Allen belt is a plasma trapped within the magnetic field of the earth, whose magnetic poles reflect it like mirrors.

At Livermore, several major research tools have been devised to study the anatomy and behavior of hot plasma confined by a magnetic field. These include experiments carried out in doughnut-shaped chambers, the "toroidal confinement experiments," and the Astron, in which a cloud of circling high-energy electrons, shaped like a flat ring and carrying a heavy electrical current, is to produce, in combination with the field that confines them, an unusual kind of magnetic bottle. Other devices are the "mirror machines," one of which is the Adiabatic Low-energy Injection Containment Experiment, which, of course, is ALICE

All these experiments are constantly being modified and improved. In many cases, the extremely advanced technology they have spawned—the ultra vacuums, the extreme cleanliness, and the attainment of a plasma of 200,000,000°C within chamber walls of temperatures close to absolute zero—have been borrowed for space research.

Here the "heart" of ALICE is removed for modification. A magnet coil in the improbable shape of the seam on a baseball was found excellent for producing a deep magnetic well in which hot plasma can be more stably confined. But this coil, even when immersed in liquid nitrogen at −195°C, demands 5,000,000 watts of power to energize it, and therefore pulses can be sent through it only intermittently.

In a recent modification of ALICE known as "Baby Baseball," the coil, composed of one of the new superconductors (zero electrical resistance) and immersed in liquid helium at −272°C, can be short-circuited upon itself, and the current will continue to flow indefinitely. Through such advances, in combination with increasingly sophisticated experiments, man's knowledge of plasma physics increases, but no man dares yet predict when a fusion reactor can be built.

Chemical Biodynamics Laboratory, Berkeley

Photosynthesis, the miraculous process by which green plants, using radiant energy, especially of the sun, convert water and carbon dioxide into the food —starches, sugars, fats, and proteins—and oxygen on which all plant and animal life ultimately depends, remained a mystery to man until the historic old sixty-inch cyclotron at Berkeley produced radioactive isotopes of carbon. In 1941, two young chemists, Samuel Ruben and Martin Kamen, both then graduate students, took the short-lived isotope carbon-11 and managed to grow, kill, separate, and analyze a plant in twenty-one minutes. This was a *tour de force*, but an isotope with a longer half-life would be more useful as a tracer. After receiving their doctorates, they took up the quest again, and experimented with carbon-14, having a half-life of 5,600 years. With the minute quantity of carbon-14 the old cyclotron could produce, Ruben made fundamental studies of photosynthesis, and published a series of epoch-making papers on the subject. A young genius already recognized as beginning a great career, he died in 1943.

During World War II, the nuclear reactors producing plutonium at Hanford, Washington, also produced, as a fission by-product, significant amounts of carbon-14. In 1945, Melvin Calvin, a young associate professor of chemistry, who, before the war, had worked with

Gilbert Lewis on the color of organic substances and the nature of chlorophyl, came to Ernest Lawrence and proposed to carry on the research in photosynthesis which Ruben at his death left unfinished. Lawrence enthusiastically approved and gave not only his support, but, a month after hostilities ceased in Japan, room in the old Radiation Laboratory where Calvin could work in complete freedom. "Just get some good work done," said Lawrence.

The old Radiation Laboratory was open, so that variously charged particles accelerated in the circular cyclotron could be deflected from targets for analysis and experiment. The group of scientists working around its perimeter were constantly meeting and discussing their latest findings. In this stimulating atmosphere, Calvin and the interdisciplinary group he gathered around him pursued through all its complexity the mystery of photosynthesis. The basic procedure was simple: feed radioactive carbon dioxide to the chlorophyl-containing cell—mostly in plants such as algae or spinach—allow it to continue photosynthesis for a certain time, kill it, and then, by depositing it along the long rim of a sheet of paper and passing a solvent across it, separate it layer by layer. The paper, laid on photographic film, then exposed itself and permitted identification of the

Chemical Biodynamics Laboratory, Berkeley

Completed in 1963, this new laboratory was designed by Calvin to function like the old Radiation Laboratory, where groups working on the perimeter continually met near the center to discuss their different discoveries.

Melvin Calvin, Director, Laboratory of Chemical Biodynamics

Nobel Laureate Calvin is developing a biochemical laboratory, capable of detecting life, to be sent by space vehicles among the planets. Eagerly he awaits the voyage of Project Apollo which will bring back to the earth rock from the moon.

various compounds where radiocarbon was lodged at the moment of death. Slowly, painstakingly, with daring imagination, Calvin and his group plotted the carbon cycle through some fifteen biochemical steps. In 1961, Calvin received the Nobel Prize "for his investigations of how plants absorb carbon dioxide, that is, the path of carbon in photosynthesis."

For Calvin and his group, solving the mystery of carbon assimilation in photosynthesis was only the beginning: now they began work on a still greater mystery and miracle, the origin of life. In all living things, the architecture of the hydrocarbons within the molecule are the same. Forms developed enough to leave hard fossils in the rocks are only six hundred million years old. Calvin and his group have found hydrocarbon-containing molecules in terrestial rocks three billion years old, and they have also found them in meteorites, though they question whether these might not have been contaminated on entering the earth's atmosphere. The age of the earth is currently estimated at four and a half billion years; were one and a half billion years long enough for the sun, the sea, and the atmosphere to evolve between them the marvelous chemistry of life? What, then, was Genesis —a sudden miracle, possible only on planets similar to earth, or was it implicit in the cosmic dust of which the universe was born?

Institute of Geophysics and Planetary Physics

Institute of Geophysics and Planetary Physics, Los Angeles

Willard F. Libby, professor of chemistry and director of the state-wide institute, received the Nobel Prize in 1960 "for his method of using carbon-14 as a measurement of time in archaeology, geology, geophysics and other sciences." Generated by cosmic rays, radiocarbon is absorbed by all living matter up to the moment of its death. Carbon-14 then begins its slow decay through its half-life of 5,730 years. It has helped to date the age of the Lascaux caves and of neolithic man in Africa, and to correlate the Babylonian and Christian calendars.

Institute of Geophysics and Planetary Physics, La Jolla

Walter H. Munk, professor of geophysics, associate director of the institute, and director of its laboratories at La Jolla, has contributed to our knowledge of waves and currents, the rotation of the earth, and tides in the deep sea. His analysis of the seismic waves caused by earthquakes has led to the detection of atomic explosions underground.

To bring the full force of contemporary science to bear in the study of this planet earth, its oceans, and its atmosphere, was the original purpose of the Institute of Geophysics when, in 1946, the Regents and President Sproul approved its establishment as a state-wide unit of coordinated research. Geophysics was then a new field, and few universities in this country recognized the need for so broad an approach. At the University of California, however, programs with wide-ranging interests already existed at Berkeley, Los Angeles, and La Jolla, and the astonishing advances possible with a multi-disciplinary group had been dramatically demonstrated by such predecessors as the Scripps Institution of Oceanography and the Lawrence Radiation Laboratory.

The scope of the new institute captured the imagination of the scientists who were asked to join; so did the prospect of pursuing fundamental research with a brilliant, informal group of colleagues and graduate students in close proximity to the great range of natural phenomena California offers.

At first, the Institute of Geophysics focused its powers on the earth alone, seeking to understand the dynamics of waves and tides, of earthquakes and volcanos, of the origin of metals and the deformation of rocks under heat and pressure, and of the relation between the earth's magnetic field and its molten core. More and more the answers seemed to lead up through the atmosphere and beyond, to the sun, the moon, the other planets, and the space between them. The growth of atmospheric research and the intense activity of several members who were on the faculty at Scripps pointed up the need for a distinct branch of the institute, as well as a new laboratory at La Jolla. In 1960, the Regents approved incorporating "and Planetary Physics" into the institute's title.

Carbon-14 Laboratory

Dating by radiocarbon is now a research technique in wide use. At Scripps Institution, the age of seawater determined by carbon-14 dating has helped to determine the overall speed of deep-water movements in the oceans. Here George S. Bien, specialist in chemistry, prepares wood from a bristle-cone pine of known age to determine whether there is any discrepancy between the chronological age of the tree and its radiocarbon age.

Two years later, the many-faceted space program at the Los Angeles campus was coordinated under the institute, both as an administrative unit and as a logical extension of its far-reaching purposes. Fundamental research and training of graduate students to investigate new ideas and creative approaches are the institute's primary aims. Students may enroll in any of the following departments: astronomy, chemistry, geology, mathematics, meteorology, physics, or planetary and space physics. Medicine, biology, and engineering science are closely related in many space projects. The institute continues to expand its facilities and develop special laboratories such as the Isotope Laboratory, wherein the counting equipment is so sensitive that living human tissues can be analyzed for carbon-14 content;

the Seismological Laboratory, where seismic models to study mathematically intractable problems have been developed; the High Pressure/High Temperature Laboratory; and others devoted to rock deformation, marine gravity, geochronology, biogeochemistry, and meteorite research. The institute has never permitted a major research effort to develop unless it can serve as a vehicle for graduate research.

On every campus of the University of California, there are undergraduates learning the basic skills and sciences of space. On several campuses, there are groups of faculty members drawn together by their common interest in space; under their direction, graduate students work out new instruments and techniques, send up balloons, rockets, and satellites, and assess and analyze the data these send back. The Space Sciences Laboratory at Berkeley, founded in 1959, has brought together faculty from many departments and disciplines, such as astronomy, physiology, engineering, molecular biology, and the social sciences. One of its main interests is the application of the superb technologies, materials, and systems developed through space research to urban problems and many other aspects of our daily life on earth.

Plasma Torch, Space Science Center, Los Angeles

The study of plasmas, or ionized gases, is essential to space research, since nearly all matter in the universe exists only in plasma form, and all high temperatures, on earth or elsewhere, involve the production and control of plasmas. Here, a graduate student observes, through a coarse protective mesh, the behavior of argon, ionized by electricity, within a magnetically controlled field.

Space Sciences

Man, at the beginning of the Space Age, is entering a phase no less momentous than when, some half billion years ago, his remote ancestors looked up through the shallow seas at the tremendous light above, and slowly, mutation by mutation, learned to live and move in that strange upper world. Now, from the shelter of earth's atmosphere, man is precipitating himself into outer space. Out there, he is convinced, lie answers to questions as ancient as his wonder and his first dim, questioning thought. Can he endure the terrible conditions of a long space flight? On the moon, on Mars, on Venus, can he learn to live, think, move, work? The marvelous and complex satellites he sends to orbit the earth and voyage through space to circle other planets can observe and report only what they were programmed to do by earth-bound men. The discoverer in space must still be man himself.

Foremost among those probing the immense unknown of space are the universities, training the scientists and the engineers, devising the instruments, analyzing the data, recreating on earth space conditions for experiment, and illuminating new courses for others to follow. Even more than other agencies, the universities are eager for the ultimate result of all this questing: knowledge. Is there a major scientific laboratory on earth today which is not hoping for a piece of the moon?

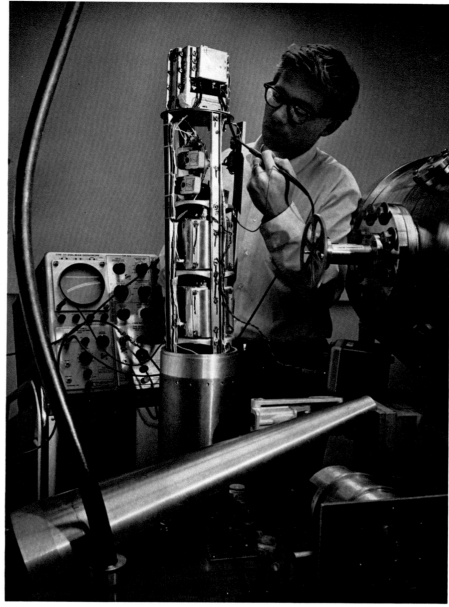

Space Sciences Laboratory, Berkeley
Graduate student of the Sounding Rocket Group adjusts the "payload" instrumentation which fits into the nose cone of a high-altitude rocket.

Electron Diffraction Pattern from Silicon Single Crystal with (III) Plane Perpendicular to Electron Beam. Inorganic Materials Research Division, Lawrence Radiation Laboratory, Berkeley

Silicon, identical in crystalline structure with diamond, is the base for many plastics that can resist both extremely low and extremely high temperatures. *Inorganic Materials Research Division photograph by G. Thomas*

IV THE UNIVERSITY AND THE LAND

The Agricultural Extension Service

When California was still a month by ship and a week by train from the rest of the nation, the University became deeply concerned for its isolated people and their means of livelihood. Educating agriculturists on campus was by itself not enough; the University began to go to the lonely ranches and little towns to identify farm problems and to help solve them. In 1874, Eugene W. Hilgard, one of the nation's great geologists and soil chemists, joined the faculty at Berkeley to build up the College of Agriculture. When, in 1891, federal funds for extension of agricultural knowledge became available, speakers from the college went about holding Farmers' Institutes all over the state. Where the new strains and techniques advocated by the University were tried, the grain grew higher, the orchards were laden down with more and finer fruit, and the lambs and beeves weighed heavier at market time.

By 1900, the Farmers' Institutes were considered "a larger classroom of the University." Farmers were involved in research, consulting with University specialists and reporting their findings at conferences. Already growers were petitioning the University to set up field stations to study their particular problems. Often they raised the necessary funds and lent their own lands and labor to the experiments.

From 1908 to 1912, the University ran "a college on wheels"—trains loaded with agricultural exhibits, lecturers, and demonstrations. Hundreds of thousands flocked to way stations and whistle stops to see. In 1914, federal funds were made available for agricultural extension work in land grant colleges throughout the nation. By that time, four counties in California had already set up offices of their own in connection with the University.

Today, offices of the University Agricultural Extension Service are in fifty-six of California's fifty-eight counties. Farm advisors are staff members of the University, but the service also involves cooperation and support from federal, state, and county governments. County farm advisors and Extension specialists often hold high academic degrees in such sciences as entomology, plant pathology, or agronomy and have, in addition, years of experience with the problems of farmers.

Their advice is available to any rancher, packer, processor, banker—whoever is interested in agriculture. Home advisors, who once worked only with the farmer's wife, now counsel professional groups and consumers. Housewives may consult with them on nutrition, child care, managing income, and improving the home. County staff members and statewide specialists may be found in many places during the course of a day and a night—in a peach orchard, where the ripening fruit is threatened by an insect invasion; at a 4-H Club meeting or a training conference; discussing land use with a planning commission; advising a processing plant on quality control; or in the role of liaison between the farmer and the University's agricultural scientists—taking part in a research conference, harvesting an experimental plot, or computer-analyzing the results.

Sheep ranch near Rio Vista

Agricultural Experiment Station, Davis

An old silo, a small research laboratory, and a few barns, sheds, and greenhouses are the relics of the scientific saga which, through an experimental farm and a statewide network of field stations and test plantings, has revolutionized California's agriculture.

The miles-long rows and furrows across vast valleys; the machines that tend them; many of the more than two hundred crops worth more than three billion dollars yearly; and the new stature of the farmer in science, business, and economics have all been developed with the help and guidance of the University and its statewide Agricultural Experiment Station, which is now concentrated on three campuses and in a dozen or more field stations.

The Davis campus was established in 1905 as the University Farm, its original purpose being to improve dairy standards. Research in animal husbandry and the devising of new machines for processing milk,

butter, and cream were soon supplemented by other aspects of agricultural research. Professors began coming from the bay climate of Berkeley to test new crops and techniques on these wide, hot, fertile plains. Students in the College of Agriculture came here to learn by experience as well as by theory. There was more and more to learn as irrigation opened the inland valleys, and machines went on replacing hands and horses. Fast trains and then trucks and planes made it possible to reach markets in the East, if fresh fruits and vegetables were picked at the right moment, painstakingly packed, and shipped immediately.

Canneries and freezing plants later burgeoned along the valleys, as an ever-growing share of the state's agricultural bounty was processed. These industries called for research. Food technology, agricultural engineering, and economic and business administration became essential additions to the more traditional agricultural sciences and skills taught at Davis.

Haying, Davis, 1931

Old Silo, Davis

Citrus Research Center and Agricultural Experiment Station, Riverside

The Citrus Experiment Station was established in 1907 to meet the research needs of growers trying to raise oranges, lemons, and grapefruit in semi-arid southern California. From the slopes of Mount Rubidoux, the first small research laboratory looked down on arid plains and hills where one good rain brought forth a quickening green and, almost overnight, thousands of flowers. University scientists were faced with many problems: how to get enough water to soak the ground deeply in the spring, and when and how to use it around the year; how to control pests and guard against frosts; what to add to the rich desert soil to encourage the growth of more and better fruit; how to pack the glowing harvest for long journeys; and what to do with the small, but delicious, culls.

University and other scientists searched Egypt, Palestine, Italy, Greece, and other countries to find the noblest strains of what the Greeks knew as the golden apples of the Hesperides. None of the citrus station's many attempts to improve these great natural mutant oranges has as yet resulted in a finer fruit, although other citrus varieties have been improved by hybridization.

The University, in learning how to grow citrus and other fruits, such as avocados and peaches, under California conditions, found itself involved in entomology and biological pest control, in pesticides and agronomy, in hydrology and hydroponics, and, in the 1940's, in air pollution research. Berkeley, Davis, and Riverside have become world-famous centers for agricultural research and innovations. They have been such magnets for students and scientists that, in many of the developing nations of the world, the highest agricultural officials hold post-graduate degrees from the University of California.

New Citrus Orchards, near Riverside

A vast acreage planned by the Church of Latter Day Saints, these orchards were planted with strains of citrus and methods of irrigation and fertilization recommended by University specialists at Riverside.

Preplanting Fumigation of Soil, Salinas Valley

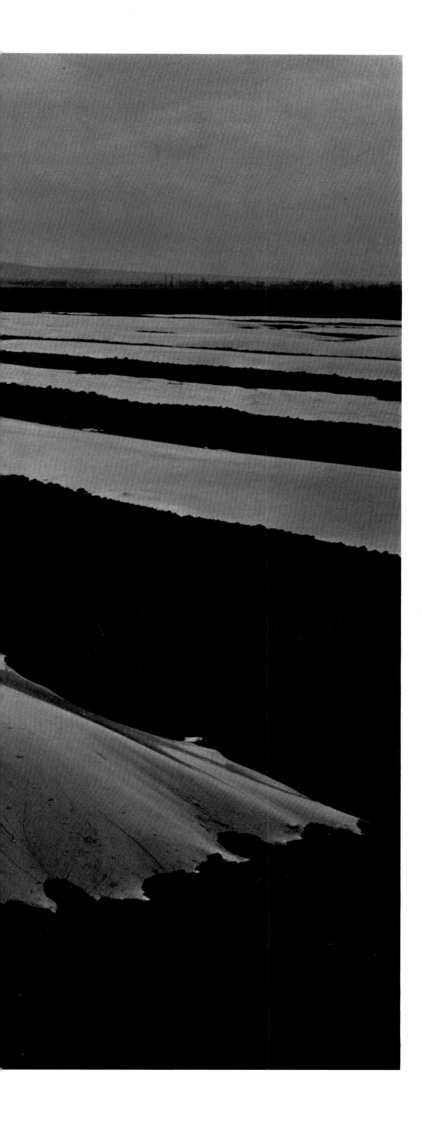

Salinas Valley

Twenty-one major crops are grown in the Salinas Valley, including strawberries, broccoli, carrots, sugar beets, wheat, and one of every four heads of lettuce sold in the United States. Some growers raise three crops a year from the same acreage. Throughout the valley, furrows are a standard two rows to eighty inches, so that tractor-mounted machines for pest control, fertilizing, and harvesting can be used interchangeably. These machines generally are owned by service companies and operated by specialists. This type of agriculture, with its flexible, cooperative, and highly organized systems, has developed in the Salinas Valley with research, planning, and advice from the local University Agricultural Extension office.

University Agricultural Extension Director for Monterey County, John W. Huffman

Pear Orchard, Department of Pomology, Davis

The desired pollen is carefully applied with a brush to each blossom; then the branch is covered to prevent bees from creating undesired hybrids. Such experiments lead to developing species better suited to a particular soil, climate, or method of cultivation.

Agricultural Research

Confronted by one of the many complex problems emerging from modern agriculture, a farm advisor may, if necessary, consult with whatever group of University specialists he thinks might be most effective in finding a solution. A pest problem might involve an agronomist, a pathologist, an entomologist, and a geneticist. A food processing problem might call for a food scientist and an engineer. A water supply problem might need a hydrologist, a soils physicist, and an economist. If consultation fails to bring forth an immediate solution, the scientists and the University Agricultural Extension experts may meet with local growers to analyze the problem and see what research by the University is necessary.

Every year, the University's research findings save growers from costly losses and multiply their capacity to produce—benefits which finally are reaped by consumers in the form of better and more plentiful food. The net increase in agricultural income annually surpasses what the state has paid for agricultural research in all the years since the University was founded.

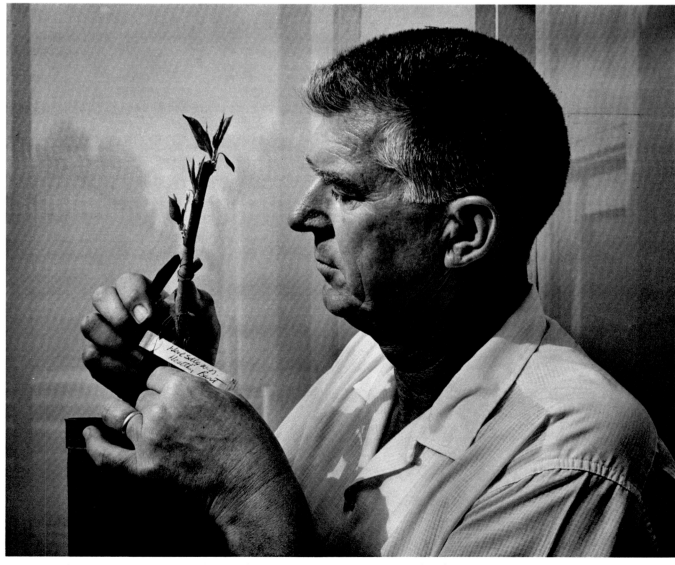

Plant Pathology, Davis. George Nyland makes a graft to test the presence of a plant virus.

The Water Resources Center

Water is crucial in California. Summer is dry. Fogs cool the northern coast, and thunderstorms tower now and then over the mountains, but otherwise little rain falls from early spring to late fall. Then, in November perhaps, great storms sweep in from the Pacific, water rushes down dry creek beds, the tawny hills turn green, and the snow mass deepens and gleams on the Sierra Nevada. Yet Northern California may be flooded while Southern California parches. On these winter rains and snows, life in California depends for the coming year.

Householders measure their water needs by the gallon, industries by the thousands of gallons, but ranchers estimate by acre-feet—the 325,000 gallons needed to cover an acre with water a foot deep. About ninety per cent of all water used in California goes onto crops. To locate underground waters for wells and pumps, as in the Salinas and San Joaquin Valleys; to transfer water by canals from Northern to Southern California, supplementing it with water from the Colorado River; and to solve the many complex difficulties attendant on building huge dams and storage reservoirs are problems demanding constant research and experiment. Above all, as more water is needed, new sources must be found. In 1951, the University began studies in seawater conversion.

In 1956, the state turned most of its huge, bewildering, and constantly expanding water research problems over to the University. The Water Resources Center was established in 1957 to coordinate and encourage such studies; seldom conducting research on its own, it allocates funds to appropriate departments of the University for specific investigations.

To determine what quality of water is needed for what purpose; to increase runoff and the replenishment of underground water; to keep pesticides, nitrates, and other pollutants from entering water systems; to reclaim and purify used water; to devise effective but inexpensive ways of converting seawater into pure or at least usable water; to prevent serious losses by evaporation of water in desert reservoirs—these are a few of the problems the Water Resources Center is currently pursuing.

Experimental Spillway, Davis

Spring Irrigation, Salinas Valley

Entomologist, Riverside

Lyle Gaston, assistant chemist, is working on problems of
chemical communication among insects.

Biological Controls, Riverside

Into the endlessly fascinating sub-world of insects, experts in biological or chemical control must often enter, waging war. Large plantings of some species of fruit, vegetable, or forage, hitherto rare in the ecology, invite some otherwise inoffensive insect to multiply into devastating hordes. Stagnant water from irrigation is perfect for breeding midges and mosquitoes. Every large disturbance of the ecology causes turmoil among insects. When birds, other insects, and insect diseases can no longer keep an economic balance, entomologists then study the troubling insect with even more intensity than before. What are its natural enemies? Is there somewhere another insect, or life in any form, which preys on this insect and *no other*? University scientists range the world over, looking for such prey-predator relationships. When they think they have found a possible parasite or predator, they bring it back, breed it, and investigate its efficiency and whatever side effects it might have on other aspects of life. They do not release it for general use until they are sure that the newcomer itself cannot become as devastating as its prey.

Such biological controls, often as simple as importing a certain ladybug to eat aphids, are most effective in areas where cooperating farmers agree on their usefulness and protect them as much as possible; healthy orchards have been thus achieved without insecticides. But in other areas, and against the majority of pests, insecticides still play an important role. University scientists work to make them safer, more selective, and more efficient; the scientists also analyze their occasionally appalling side effects, including contaminated soil, water, wildlife, and birds as remote as Antarctic penguins. Even man may become a victim, if he mishandles insecticides.

Discovering ways of decreasing pests by means other than poison or predators also interests the researchers. For instance, by synthesizing the sex signals and allures—pheromones—of certain moths, the male can be trapped to prevent mating. Another means of control is by management: for example, the lygus bug

Ph.D. in Entomology, Riverside
Sudha Rho received her degree for research in problems of biological control vital to her native India. She has already returned to apply her knowledge toward solving her country's food shortages.

breeds in the foothills, and, when those surroundings grow hot, moves to greener pastures, with a preference for alfalfa. In the alfalfa fields, these pests are at home with their natural enemies, who keep them to a reasonable balance. But when the alfalfa is cut, they move on to the cotton fields, where they do enormous damage. A simple solution was suggested by University researchers: cut alfalfa in strips at different times; these insects, who do not damage the alfalfa crop, shift from the cut strip to the standing strip, and never move on to the cotton.

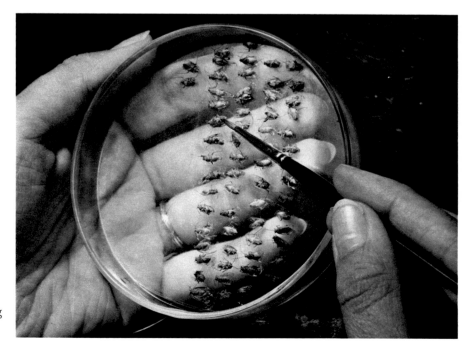

Technician, Riverside
Paintbrushes prove more delicate than tweezers in handling small forms of life.

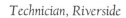

Broccoli Harvester, Salinas Valley

In many crops, stoop labor is vanishing. The bag and the basket are being replaced by conveyor belts, hoists, and trucks. This broccoli harvester, designed by a graduate of the University of California School of Engineering, is a "man-aid."

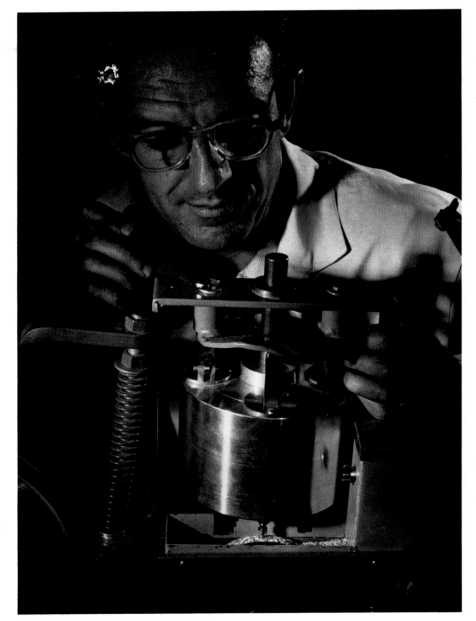

Agricultural Engineering, Davis

George Giannini, technician, works on the prototype of a lettuce-seed planter which has reduced the hand labor of thinning.

Mechanization

The dwindling supply and rising costs of agricultural hand labor have spurred mechanization. But to produce even one machine that supplants the human hand may take not only years of experiment by engineers, but also may require geneticists to find or develop a fruit with a tougher skin or a shape which rolls, and growers to try new techniques of planting or training. And when all this work is reasonably perfected, it takes a courageous group of farmers to try a new machine, a new system, and a new crop simultaneously.

Lettuce Picker, Salinas Valley

Farm advisor Bill Huffman, Jack Bias, executive vice-president of the local growers' association, and Tom Merrill, farmer, all graduates of the University of California, discuss a lettuce harvester invented by the agricultural engineering department at Davis. With this machine, one man will replace perhaps a dozen men. An electronic sensor determines the maturity of the lettuce head, a curved paddle grasps it, a knife cuts the stem, and a conveyor belt moves the lettuce to the waiting truck.

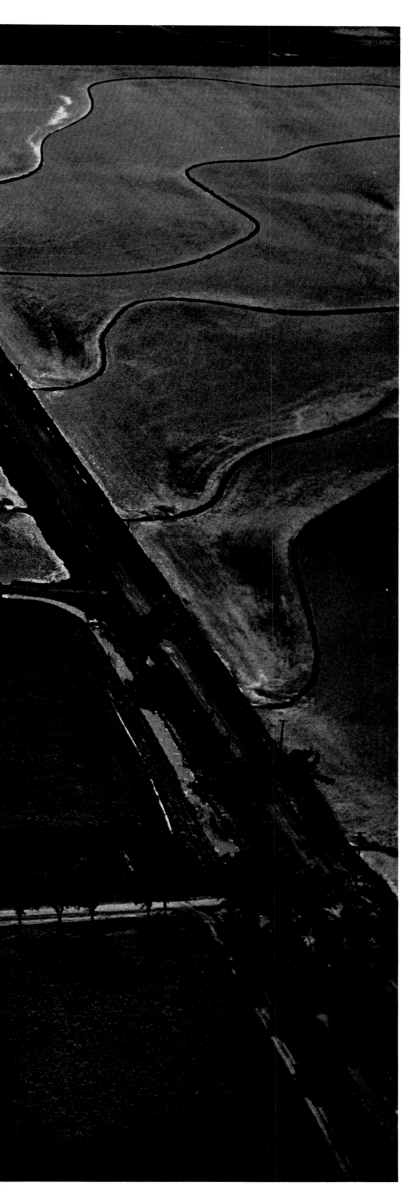

Rice

Rice is basic to the diet of more than half the people in the world. Here in the Sacramento Valley, through the warm, shallow water between these low levees lift the first sprouts of a rice crop that will yield more than 5,500 pounds of rice per acre—an average greater than anywhere else in the world.

Research has been the key to this success. The Rice Experiment Station, a cooperative venture of the University, the federal government, and the growers, was established in the Sacramento Valley in 1912 and has been maintained through funds raised by the industry. Here scientists have found the varieties best adapted to the region, have helped work out cultivation techniques such as specialized herbicides for weed control, and have helped to make rice the most highly mechanized crop in California.

In other parts of the world, four hundred to nine hundred man-hours are needed per acre of rice; here only seven and one half man-hours per acre are necessary. Seeding and spraying are done with planes; only one man is needed to guide the giant harvesters. The Sacramento River, which irrigates these fields, also bears rice-laden ships to the Pacific and thence to Asia, Africa, and all parts of the world.

Farm in the rice fields, Sacramento Valley

Enologist in the Agricultural Experiment Station

Maynard A. Amerine, professor of enology at Davis, tests the sugar content of ripening grapes. Originally a plant physiologist, Amerine has become an international authority on wines and brandies in every stage of their production, from the vine and the climate to the final tasting. He has done biochemical research and has studied methods of wine-making in Portugal, Spain, France, Italy, Germany, Russia, Yugoslavia, and Japan. His published works include scientific studies, production manuals, textbooks, histories of wine and its appreciation, and comprehensive bibliographies of viticulture and enology. The department he and his colleagues have developed at Davis is widely considered a major world center of enological research.

Wine Cellar, Department of Enology, Davis

Each lot of bottles represents a carefully controlled and recorded experiment. Enologist Amerine calls this cellar "the only university library in the world that is entirely in bottles."

New Vineyard, Salinas Valley

Wine

Winemaking in California began with the Spanish Californians who used grapes from vines they had planted in mission gardens. Half a century later, families from Germany, Italy, France, Switzerland, and other European countries brought cuttings of noble grapes, set them out on the wild hillsides, and began the commercial wine industry. But traditional skills were not enough to ensure fine wines in a strange country, and both vineyardists and wine makers often sought the aid of the University in finding a disease-resistant rootstock, for example, or improved strains of budwood, or better techniques of storing, filtering, and bottling.

California has many climates, from alpine to subtropic. Maynard Amerine and his colleague, Albert J. Winkler, have divided those favorable to wine grapes into five regions, from cool to hot. In

Regions One and Two, cool and near the coast, grow the light-bearing varieties from whose small grapes come the most distinguished dry table wines. Vines which flourish in the heat bear heavily: from their huge clusters come standard wines and sweet dessert wines.

Before deciding on this site near the Pinnacles, the wine-maker asked the advice of the Department of Viticulture and Enology at Davis. Soil and water were analyzed; their temperatures and that of the air and the amount of sunlight throughout the year were recorded. This part of the Salinas Valley was then designated as Region Two, prime for fine dry table wines. The department recommended five varieties and will continue to observe the young vines for at least seven years.

Dry Lands Research Institute

One half of the world's lands suffers from the effects of aridity, yet upon them one third of its population depends for sustenance.

Deserts occur in eroding country. Rocks crack and crumble under intense heat and sudden frosts; cloudbursts suddenly roar down gulches, fronted by avalanches of boulders and brush. The rivers in flood are heavy with silts and salts, building up deposits of rich soil sometimes a mile or more in depth; but the rivers dry up, if uncontrolled, before they have leached the salts below the reach of roots. When their waters are used for irrigation, the salts accumulate, rising with the water table until they kill almost all plants and appear on the surface. Salt crusts the once-fertile lands of many vanished civilizations in Africa, the near East, and the Orient.
California's success in coping with this immemorial curse, especially in the Coachella and Imperial Valleys, has drawn scientists and graduate students from counties that are heirs to the ancient poisoned lands, as well as from developing nations who must farm the virgin desert if they are to survive. The work in these valleys seemed to a Riverside campus committee only the beginning of what research could accomplish in the arid lands. They proposed a University-wide institute whose purposes would be to study arid lands around the world; to discover how deserts are formed, and how life conforms and contributes; to survey what happens when man introduces new technologies, plantations, and urban developments; to select, breed, and improve plants and animals to meet the demands of new environments; and to determine the vital balance between the demands of man and those of the wilderness on whose undisturbed functions life, water, soil, and air depend.

The Dry Lands Research Institute, centering in Riverside, was established by the Regents in 1963, and funded by grants from the Rockefeller Foundation. Already the institute has conducted study tours of North and East Africa, the Near East, the Mediterranean Region, and Western South America, and has helped graduate students from Argentina, Australia, Brazil, Cyprus, Egypt, India, Iran, Israel, Jordan, Lebanon, Sudan, Syria, Turkey, West Pakistan, and the United States, with its own vast arid lands in the West.

Thunderheads, Anza-Borrego Desert

Cotton field, evening sandstorm, Coachella Valley

Cotton, both the long staple Egyptian, and the short staple Acala, is so well adapted to desert conditions that it grows well even in saline and alkaline soils, as long as it has water. Cotton is the largest cash crop in California, and there are those who claim California grows more cotton than Texas.

Desert Agriculture

Wind and salt, heat and drought, are the conditions a farmer faces in the desert. In 1900, the Coachella and Imperial Valleys were still the western reaches of the brutal and beautiful Colorado Desert; they sloped down to the Salton Sink, which, at 273 feet below sea level, was almost as low and salt-encrusted as its neighbor, Death Valley. In 1901, water was brought in by canal from the Colorado River, and farmers discovered that on these rich soils crops could be grown the year around, for harvesting when no other region could compete. Flood control of such powerful rivers as the Colorado was not then well understood. When in 1904 the floods began rising, too much water was diverted to the Imperial Valley. The floods, cresting along the canal, swept over its banks and down into the great inland basin, where, during the next two years, they created the Salton Sea. Farmers on the surrounding lands found in their midst a shrinking lake, which, by the time it formed its permanent shoreline, was saltier than the ocean.

For a few more years, the crops were magnificent. Then field crops showed bald spots, and orchards withered. Salt crusts, black or white, began to appear on the surface. Analysis proved that Colorado River water contains a ton of salts in every acre-foot, and most irrigated crops were receiving five or more tons a year on every acre. Most of this water-borne burden of salt drained off into the Salton Sea or was leached downward; but that which remained in the root zone could be deadly to growing plants.

As early as 1912, the University was testing in the Imperial Valley which fruits, vegetables, and forage crops could endure the wind, the salt, and the heat. Windbreaks were devised—palm fronds, cover crops, tamarisks, and paper caps. Salt-tolerant varieties that flourished in the heat were found. But there remained the problem of how to control the salts, which became more concentrated with every irrigation.

The University's current solution is to begin with a test planting of barley, one of the most salt tolerant crops, and hope that the irrigation water will flush the soil salts downward. But if the sub-surface water rises and crop yields remain sparse, then tile drains will be laid in gravel seven feet down; if necessary, surface ponds will be created among low levees, and will be filled with standing water to leach the salt down to the pipes that bear it to the Salton Sea.

Grapefruit Harvest, Coachella Valley

Grapefruit, lemons, limes, tangerines, and Valencia oranges now flourish in this valley. So do fine table grapes, such as Thompson Seedless, Cardinal, and several varieties developed by the University, such as Perlette and the colored Beauty Seedless, which are harvested here in June and July when no other region can supply the markets of the United States.

Dates

Date palms are an immemorial symbol of life in the desert. Untold generations of men have watered them, climbed them to dethorn and prune, to pollenize and to pick, have eaten of their rich fruit, and lived and died gratefully in their shade. In the Coachella Valley, citrus orchards are sometimes planted between them; their majestic crests shield the more tender fruits and blossoms from frost. They are tolerant of salt, they flourish in dry air and hot sun, and they require a lot of water. Until a few years ago, in the Coachella Valley, they were tended by crowds of singing Mexicans. University agricultural engineers worked with growers and manufacturers to mechanize the process of harvest. Now men on moving platforms pass among the palms, pruning, pollenizing, putting paper hoods over the young clusters to protect them from the birds, and at harvest time, cutting the heavy bunches of dates.

Date Palm Grove during irrigation, Coachella Valley

Wildland Research Center

Sixty-five millions of California's hundred million acres are wildlands—forest, grasslands, sagebrush, chaparral, and alpine heights. From these come ninety-seven per cent of California's water, much of it pure, high quality water. In coastal canyons and on the slopes and ridges of the Sierra Nevada grow the forests which provide timber, plywood, paper, wood and charcoal. On grassy uplands dotted with oaks graze the cattle and sheep from which come beef and lamb, wool and leather. Deer browse the valleys and the heights, and ducks nest in the marshes, trout leap in the lakes, and salmon battle swift streams to reach their spawning grounds. Until nearly a century ago, the wildlands were considered inexhaustible—the wildlife, the wild range, the forests rising ridge after ridge toward the Pacific. Then the signs of neglect and abuse appeared—thousands of acres of stumps; eroding watersheds caused by destructive mining and logging, floods, and wildfires; hills grazed dry, minutely terraced by hooves, breaking under the winter rains; birds, beasts, and fishes in danger of extinction.

From its founding in 1914, the Division of Forestry at the University has been concerned with all the wildlands, in managing them in their interaction so that these great resources shall not only be conserved, but, where necessary, improved to meet all humanity's needs—not only wood and water, range and recreation, but also beauty. By 1946, now organized as the School of Forestry, its program recognized all branches of wildland management. Then, as the conflicting demands of an exploding population for food, housing, clothing, water, and recreation increased, and threatened still more seriously the vitality of the wildlands, the University in 1958 established within the Agricultural Experiment Station the Wildland Research Center, where, under the direction of the dean of forestry, researchers from more than a dozen different scientific disciplines work together to solve the many problems of the wildlands.

Near Tule Lake, Siskiyou County

Range Management

The Spanish, in the eighteenth century, seeing lush grasslands full of fat deer, antelope, and elk, turned their sheep and cattle loose to graze, rounding them up now and then for branding, shearing, and slaughtering. California became one of the great cattle countries of the world. American ranchers, too, turned their livestock loose on the wild range. The wildflowers and native grasses largely disappeared, and weeds, brought from Europe as seeds caught in the wool of sheep and the hair of cattle, began taking over the pasturelands. Chamisa, thistles, and barbed foxtail increased until hilltops from the coast ranges to the foothills of the Sierra Nevada were crowned with chaparral and oaks, cattle and sheep grew thin on the depleted and eroding range, and deer descended to attack man's crops.

In 1951, the University acquired a typical cattle ranch near Hopland, in the steep, shining, coast range country. After a period of careful observation and tabulation of the results of such ranching practices, the Division of Agricultural Sciences began to conduct experiments of many kinds aimed at improving the range and increasing meat production. From the School of Forestry at Berkeley and from many departments at Davis, researchers came to conduct experiments and demonstrations, such as the control-burning of undesirable brush, the reseeding of the range with grasses and clovers to provide yearlong forage, the management of deer, and the breeding and feeding of the earliest fat lambs for market.

Cattle Ranch, Tehama County, near Redding

Beef cattle, dairy cattle, and sheep are today the leading source of agricultural income in California. Range improvement and cross-breeding techniques for more meat are only two aspects of the enormous change urbanization has caused in livestock industries. Pasturelands shrink as the cities advance. A rancher for whom twenty good dairy cows made a living ten years ago must now, on the same land or less, manage at least a hundred cows. Mechanization, control of disease, and nutrition studies have made it possible for a single cow to produce a third more milk than she could before.

School of Forestry, Berkeley

The magnificent forests of California! Trees once widespread are now making their last stand here. The Monterey cypress, shaped by the sea wind, still clings through the centuries to rocky promontories above the surf. The bristle-cone pines, eleven thousand feet up on the shoulders of the White Mountain range, have endured storm, lightning, snow, and drought for four thousand years and more, and still, though gnarled and skeletal, put forth here and there a green twig. On the western slopes of the Sierra Nevada, around seven thousand feet, the vast, shining forests of sugar pine, ponderosa pine, white fir, and incense cedar sometimes part to reveal the towering presence of the Big Trees, *Sequoia gigantea,* twenty feet and more in diameter, immense in their baroque splendor; fire has often hollowed charcoal caves in their trunks, yet still they live, some of them three thousand years old, tapering up to crowns more than two hundred feet in the air. Taller still, often three hundred and fifty feet high, and some of them more than a thousand years old, the coast redwoods, *Sequoia sempervirens,* form a forest unforgettable for its grace and majesty and for its exquisite floor of scented duff, ferns, and flowering sorrels. Once dominant over the Northern Hemisphere, redwoods now grow naturally only in canyons near the Pacific coast, in a strip from five to twenty miles wide—"as far as the fog blows," goes the saying—and some five hundred miles long, from the Big Sur to the Oregon border.

Eugene W. Hilgard, at the University Agricultural Experiment Station, started experiments in tree planting around 1875, giving priority at first to hardwoods useful for hoe handles and axe helves; since the local oaks were limited in usefulness and Eastern hardwoods proved a conspicuous failure, he began importing species from other dry countries, such as Australia. Forestation, especially of the arid, barren mountains of Southern California, concerned him deeply. Again and again he tried to get funds for forestation programs and for a school of forestry that should be more than "economic botany" and should "look forward to centuries to come."

Forestry, a science born of necessity in deforested Europe about the time Columbus sailed, was new to the United States. Progressively, across the continent for more than two hundred years, Americans had been felling their forests for international needs as well as their own. Now they were turning to Germany, Norway, and Finland for advice, and were soon aware, with Gifford Pinchot, that the forests of northern Europe were different both in species and dynamics from most of the forests of the eastern United States. The first school of forestry, founded in 1898 at Cornell, in New York State, had little but German texts and short studies in forestry bulletins to guide them. In 1899, Benjamin Ide Wheeler, coming from Cornell to become the eighth president of the University, declared in his inaugural address: "Not only the naked hills of California but the whole western slope of the continent call for a special study of the forest problem. A school of forestry is an earnest and instant need."

Wheeler tried repeatedly to get funds for a school of forestry from the legislature and from the lumber industry. An undergraduate Forestry Club gathered the ammunition and barrage of letters that finally, in 1913, secured the necessary financial support from the legislature for a school of forestry at the University.

The first chief of the Division of Forestry was Walter Mulford. Although he knew from his work at Cornell and Michigan only the Eastern forests, he saw California as a whole to be managed, in all its diversity for all the diversity of man's needs, for generations to come. The forester, in his concept, was not merely a grower of trees. Scientists working to understand the reciprocals between logging and renewal, the role of fire and flood in the regeneration of the wildlands, the development of means to fight wildfires and prevent wild floods, the study of the influence of the forest on the climates around and below it, the first textbooks dealing with range management and with forest influences, the study of snow melt and the hydrology of brushlands—these are among the contributions made by the School of Forestry faculty under the continuing inspiration of Walter Mulford. Alumni of the school are now scattered over all the continents, in education, in private industry, and in government service.

Ponderosa Pines, Sierra Nevada

The laboratory of wildland research is the outdoors of California. It may be lumber company land, or part of a national forest, or a state or national park. Many problems, however, call for control and study over many decades; the University owns tracts of several different types of forests, such as Blodgett Forest in El Dorado County, where experiments in many systems of land management are carried out in a typical Sierra Nevada forest. Whitaker's Forest, 320 acres in the southern Sierra, close to Kings Canyon-Sequoia National Parks, contains magnificent groves of both old-growth and new-growth *Sequoia gigantea.* Here foresters and landscape architects work together clearing thickets of white fir and incense cedar, to make the forest less vulnerable to fire, to open up park-like vistas of the virgin sequoias, and to attain—and maintain—the beauty of such groves as first seen and described by John Muir and other early explorers.

University Forestry Camp, Plumas County

Rudolf F. Grah, professor of forestry, explains to summer camp students the principles of selective logging; mature trees, whose growth has slowed, are removed to give sun, space, and soil to young growth. An old-growth forest of yellow pine and mixed conifers surrounds the school: here and in cutover lands nearby which are being reforested, students acquire the actual field practice required by the School of Forestry degree.

The Forest Products Laboratory

The early loggers, intent on boards and timbers, used less than half the tree. Stumps, tops, and branches were left in the forest; bark, slabs, trimmings, and sawdust were burned at the sawmills. Smoke from their burners dimmed the valleys, and wildfires, igniting in dry litter, raged over thousands of acres of forest. Such waste was considered inevitable; there was no economically feasible use for slash.

Today the needs and interest of the forest products industries demand that any tree harvested must, from root to needles, find economic use. Veneer and plywood, chipboard, pulp and paper, laminated timber— all these require intensive research into the physics and chemistry of various native woods. Few lumber companies can afford such staffs, and University foresters, from Walter Mulford on, urged the establishment of a laboratory within the University that should develop such uses for California's forests. The appointment of a wood chemist to the faculty was the first step; in 1951, the legislature approved the project, and four years later, in a handsome new building on the Richmond Field Station, the Forest Products Laboratory developed an intensive program of research with three main objectives: first, use of the whole tree; second, uses for native trees of previously rejected species; and, third, the discovery through pure science of potentials not yet envisaged in wood.

Industry assists, with guidance through a technical advisory council, and from time to time, makes welcome donations of funds and materials to various projects. Already the laboratory, often in cooperation with other departments of the University, such as the Departments of Chemical Engineering and Sanitary Engineering, has found uses for some seventy-five per cent of the tree: slabs and trimmings go into chipboard; sawdust is added to adhesives for plywood; bark is shredded and made into pads for packaging California fruits, soil conditioners and substitutes, and fillers for packing around oil well drills; stumps prove a source for resins and new chemical agents for medicine and agriculture. Of the neglected woods, madrone provides a beautiful veneer and short lengths for parquetry floors, tan oak a durable flooring for railroad cars, and incense cedar a fragrant casing for pencils.

Slashburners will soon be obsolete, and slash burning an unlamented memory.

Hands with Chips, Eureka

Pulp Mill, Eureka

Mountains of chips, once burned as the sole way to get rid of
them, are brought in huge trucks which are lifted up, cab and all,
to dump their contents into bins. Movable pipes spray the chips
forth, to wait until they go to be pulped and bleached for paper.
Few paper mills until recently have been built in California:
contamination of air or water by the evil-smelling effluents of the
older pulping processes has been strictly controlled by law. Now
chemists have developed processes of wood pulping that are both
more efficient and free of pollutants. In one, still experimental,
the waste material, even the water used in washing the chips,
proves to be a fertilizer rich in nitrogen.

Humboldt County

The first settlers of this region were farmers. They looked at the alluvial flats where the biggest redwoods grew and thought of rich farms, at the slopes covered with firs and redwoods and saw hills covered with sheep and cattle. They cleared the forest, sold the great logs, and began to plough and build among the stumps, assuming they would soon rot. But redwoods have miraculous powers of renewal: next year the sprouts around the stumps were taller than a man. The settlers burned them and set fire to the hills. But redwood resists fire; even from apparent charcoal, snags sprouted again, while from the trees left standing as not worth logging, seed floated copiously down to root in soil fertilized by ashes. The settlers suddenly discovered a dense carpet of seedlings springing up everywhere. Both axe and fire failed: only the plough succeeded. The settlers gave up the battle in the hills and went back to tilling the valleys.

Today, eighty to a hundred years later, these insistent seedlings are the future wealth of the region. Nearly a hundred feet high and two or three feet thick, they are ready for harvesting. Foresters trained at the University begin to mark them for selective logging, aiming to produce a mixed forest of all ages that will yield perpetually, or, when appropriate, clear cut blocks of timber and regenerate even-aged young stands. The Forest Products Laboratory continues to develop better milling techniques and new uses for all kinds of wood. The lumber companies are proud of their forests and of their industry. One spokesman said, "We own one hundred and eighty thousand acres, and we hope to live on them forever."

Second growth, Humboldt County

Pediatrics Weighing Room, Clinics Building, San Francisco
Fourth-year medical students assist the faculty and the full-
time staff in the center's fifty clinics, covering the full range of
contemporary medicine, which receive more than 208,000
patient visits a year.

V THE UNIVERSITY AND THE COMMUNITY

The Health Sciences

"We are in the midst of an authentic social revolution which subjects
our changing, urbanized culture to stresses and strains of the greatest
magnitude. The health sciences, in contributing to the search for
solutions to the problems engendered by these changes, must extend
their horizons beyond disease and beyond the individual organism. We
must contribute to and draw upon a broader knowledge of man in
health—the whole man in his total environment."

JOHN B. deC. M. SAUNDERS, M.B., Ch.B., F.R.C.S. (Edin.)
Chairman, Department of History of the Health Sciences,
School of Medicine, San Francisco

Medical education has come a very long way from the courses in "physiology, *materia medica*, midwifery, chemistry, surgery and pathology" offered by the Toland Medical College when it opened in San Francisco in 1864. A high school education, or a year's apprenticeship to some "reputable" surgeon were sufficient for entrance; two eighteen-week semesters, creditably performed, were sufficient for graduation.

Today, the enormous and constantly proliferating complexity of medicine requires an education of at least ten years, beginning with the undergraduate years at college level and the four years at medical school involving, at a minimum, study of the science and clinical applications of some twenty-five different branches, beginning with the basic biochemistry and biophysics and encompassing such fields as nuclear medicine, microbiology, genetics, embryology, obstetrics, gynecology, pediatrics, radiology, psychiatry, preventive medicine, and surgery. Then come the years of internships and residencies, and often postgraduate fellowships in the field of specialization. All this training today is needed to make a doctor. It is no longer possible for any man to master all the branches of medicine embraced by the old term, "general practitioner." It is not even possible to specialize in "eye, ear, nose and throat." Every doctor today has in some sense to be a specialist. The "family doctor" has specialized in the diagnosis and treat-

ment of a wide spectrum of common human diseases, and he monitors constantly and with a sensitive ear the avalanche of new discoveries and specifics pouring from the laboratories in numbers which increase geometrically decade by decade. Many hailed in the popular press as "miracles of modern medicine" and "wonder drugs" have proved to have dangerous side-effects and long-term consequences. Accurate diagnosis is imperative; what saves a life in a particular instance may be lethal in another. The conscientious doctor will not prescribe unless the x-rays, blood counts, cardiograms, and other tests point to a correct diagnosis. For such reasons, doctors increasingly work in teams, whose specialties extend each other. Even within these specialties, the rising pace of change in medical practice and the continuous creation of new knowledge through research make it imperative that the doctor continue his education throughout his professional life. He can never stop learning.

To meet this need, University Extension provides short courses, conferences, symposia, and two-way television discussions and demonstrations for doctors throughout the state. Many are highly specialized and technical. Others consider from many viewpoints, often national and international, problems and potentials undreamed of by the young physician more than a century ago.

Radiology Laboratory,
School of Medicine, UCLA

William N. Hanafee, M.D., Associate
Professor, chief of the x-ray laboratory
in the Health Sciences Center, and
Sherman Mellinkoff, dean of the
School of Medicine, UCLA.

167

Open Heart Operation, H. C. Moffitt Hospital, San Francisco Medical Center

The Moffitt Hospital, completed in 1955, is the largest and most comprehensive training hospital in the West. Many of the 19,000 patients the center's hospitals serve each year suffer from diseases difficult to diagnose or to treat apart from the enormous research facilities of the center's laboratories, institutes, and highly trained teams of specialists, such as those needed to perform an open heart operation. Until 1952, no one could successfully stop the human heart, open, and repair it. Now techniques and instruments of great subtlety, such as the heart-lung machines which recirculate and reoxygenate the patient's blood during the five-to-seven-hour operation, and artificial valves, such as the ball-in-cage device here being inserted, have resulted in saving hundreds of lives.

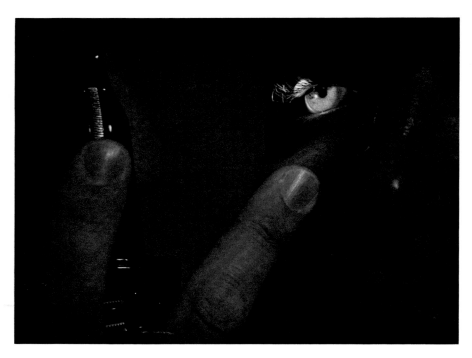

Schools of Medicine

Currently, within the University of California, there are five medical schools. At San Francisco, the school, more than a century old, is the core of the now vast medical center, with its two hospitals, fifty clinics, and pioneering research institutes. Around the school at UCLA, which opened in 1951 on a thirty-five acre tract of the southern campus, there has grown the already immense Center for the Health Sciences, with its hospital, clinics, and brilliant new research centers such as the Brain Research Institute and the Jules Stein Eye Institute. The school at UCLA has developed a new medical curriculum providing for continuous adaptation to change, with a broad choice of courses from which the student can mould his training toward his interests and plans for the future. At Davis, the new school will share with the School of Veterinary Science such extraordinary resources as the great primate colony and the long-established laboratories of toxicology, radiobiology, and ecology. In much the same way, the new school at San Diego will make use of new scientific facilities as well as the remarkable laboratories at Scripps during a highly experimental and flexible program intended to culminate in a fourth year largely free for creative research. At Irvine, medicine will center in the California College of Medicine, a recent affiliate of the University, which will move from Los Angeles and be relocated on the Irvine campus.

The new schools will be serving local hospitals and clinics long after they have established hospitals and clinics of their own. They will be initiating research projects and research centers. Because the researcher is also a teacher, he can communicate his new knowledge directly to students, interns, residents, and staffs of community hospitals. Patients thus receive the most advanced medical care. Reports of local achievements, locally tested, are communicated through University Extension programs to the state and through professional publications to physicians everywhere.

Preliminary Eye Examination,
Jules Stein Eye Institute, UCLA

"What are the functions of a school of medicine? The three basic essentials must be teaching, research and community service. The neglect of any one spells potential failure of its role. Indeed, the more that these three phases can be melded together, the greater the accomplishment of the institution will be."

WILLIAM O. REINHARDT, M.D.
Professor of Anatomy,
School of Medicine, San Francisco

"Yesterday's research is today's teaching and tomorrow's practice."

SHERMAN M. MELLINKOFF, M.D.
Dean, School of Medicine, UCLA

Laboratory Research, Langley Porter Neuropsychiatric Institute, San Francisco Medical Center

Founded in 1941, and operated jointly by the California Department of Mental Hygiene and the School of Medicine, the institute offers training to medical and nursing students, advanced fellows in psychiatry, physicians in other special fields, social workers, schoolteachers, the clergy, and rehabilitation therapy trainees. Clinical work is both inpatient, for short-term treatment of severe disorders, and outpatient, for adults and children. Two major new programs, already widely copied throughout the United States, are the care of the geriatric and the acutely disturbed at home.

School of Criminology, Berkeley

The School of Criminology at Berkeley is the only school of its kind in the United States and possibly in the world. In 1916, inspired by the need of police service candidates for training, August Vollmer, then the chief of the Berkeley Police, and Alexander M. Kidd, Boalt Professor of Law, formulated together a summer session program of study in criminology. There was grave need to probe, with the full force of the rapidly developing natural, social, and behavioral sciences, into the causes of crime and how to prevent, detect, treat, and control it. There was need to reexamine the penal code and the methods of correction. There was also, on a national scale, the growing need for men and women professionally trained in criminology to enter the Federal Probation Service, established in 1925, and the Federal Bureau of Prisons, founded in 1931, both of which work, together with the United States District Courts, to deal effectively with the offender and restore him whenever possible to social usefulness.

Vollmer and Kidd continued to give the summer sessions until 1931, when at last, in response to their proposal that a school of criminology be created, funds were allotted to establish a criminology program in the regular session, and a committee appointed to study the widely ranging needs of this new profession. Criminology at the University began as a group major in 1933, grew rapidly, and in 1950 was finally established as the school Volmer and Kidd envisaged.

Today, the school's advisory council, drawn mostly from city, county, and state officers in California, includes the attorney general, justices of the District Court of Appeals and of the Supreme Court, the chiefs of police of Berkeley and Oakland, the coroner of the city and county of San Francisco, the directors of the Department of Corrections and of the Youth Authority, and several probation officers. The faculty of the school is a "teaching community," involving professors of biochemistry, social welfare, city planning and architecture, metrology, transportation engineering, chemistry, psychiatry, psychology, political science, sociology, and toxicology, in addition to those in criminology, law, and criminalistics. The undergraduate must have already laid the basis for a broad education before he can be admitted. Increasingly, the faculty and students of the school engage in research directed to finding answers for pressing social questions. Funded by and under the aegis of foundations, private organizations, and the state and federal governments, the school designs and implements research projects of immense and immediate importance. One, still current, concerns the most effective role of the probation officer: from data compiled through the computers, a profile of the usual federal offender in such crimes as forgery and embezzlement is drawn, and shows him to be white, Protestant, a young adult, limited in education, vocational skills, and income, and frequently instable, with a history of conflict and deviance. The probation officer, who must prepare for the presiding judge the pre-sentencing report and appear with the offender before the district court, gives him meanwhile such supervision and assistance as seems required. Preliminary findings on this project seem to indicate that this assistance should not be a crutch—except in crisis—but a catalyst between the offender and the community to which, ultimately, he should return.

Another project, recently completed, centered on the question of middle class juvenile delinquency. Why, from a pleasant, suburban, affluent atmosphere of barbecue pits, swimming pools, and good schools, did adolescents develop into delinquent gangs? The "ivy-league white shoes" and the "levi pants black shoes" have little to do with each other, but they often end up officially or unofficially with their desperate parents suggesting solutions short of institutional correction. Gathering data under such circumstances involved faculty and students of the School of Criminology in pizza parlors, twenty-nine-cent hamburger drive-ins, pool rooms, ice cream palaces, skating rinks, and Little League baseball fields. Their findings resulted in a poignant picture of limbo: the adolescent, once an integral part of the family system and a source of strength and income, is today forbidden by law to work and compelled by law to continue his education, whatever his or her capacities or interests may be. They have no responsibilities to family or community, no duties to society; they are marking time until they are adults. Meanwhile they herd together and the cleavage between them and their parents is almost complete. The School of Criminology suggests that they be given responsibility and a voice in the regulation of their own conduct; that they be rescued from limbo and inducted into society, and that, for the offenders, the strategies devised by parents be made explicit and quietly put to work by the community.

Evening Discussion Group, University Extension

Schools of Law

The University now includes three schools of law on its campuses and one affiliate in San Francisco, the Hastings College of the Law. Founded in 1878 by the first chief justice of California, Serranus Clinton Hastings, who paid $100,000 into the state treasury as a starter, Hastings is the oldest law school in the West. The current chief justice is always president of its board of directors. Although Hastings clearly intended the college to be established ultimately at Berkeley, this has never happened; meeting first in Pioneer Hall, then at the Academy of Sciences, later dislodged from the City Hall by the 1906 earthquake and fire, the college moved to fifteen different locations about San Francisco before coming to rest at last in its own modern building at Hyde and McAllister Streets in 1953.

On the Berkeley campus, what is now the School of Law traces its beginnings to a course in Roman law given in 1882 by a young Latin instructor. William Carey Jones, a recent alumnus, had "read" privately for the law and passed his bar examinations, but returned to the University to teach. From Latin he turned to history, and gave courses in international law, constitutional law, and jurisprudence. By 1894 there was a Department of Jurisprudence, with Jones as its head, and by 1903, it granted its first LL.B. degrees. In 1906, Elizabeth Boalt, seeing the department's crowded condition in old North Hall, with its library down in the basement of Bacon Art and Library Building, gave $100,000 toward a law building to be named in memory of her late husband, Judge John Henry Boalt, and $50,000 more was contributed by lawyers throughout the state. The department became a school, and Jones was still its dean when he died in 1923.

When in 1951 the School of Law moved into much larger quarters, the name Boalt Hall was transferred to the new classroom wing, and the name of Garrett W. McEnerney given to the library wing whose construction he made possible. The library has been designated an official depository of all the proceedings of the United States Supreme Court since 1939 by

United States Chief Justice Earl Warren, an alumnus, and is also a depository of the proceedings of the California State Legislature. From this center, the law complex has grown to include the Earl Warren Legal Center and Manville Hall, a seven-story residence hall for law students, thus becoming the first fully self-contained living and study unit on the Berkeley campus.

The UCLA School of Law was established by the legislature in 1947, in recognition of the growing need for lawyers experienced in the legal problems of southern California. Thus, in addition to the basic curriculum, the law faculty is engaged in teaching and research concerned with the legal problems of the entertainment industry, the oil and gas industry, and of urban society in the fields of land planning, industrial relations, and the administration of criminal justice. UCLA's student lawyers frequently volunteer to serve in the defense of the criminal indigent.

At Davis, the newly developing School of Law emphasizes, especially in research and public service, problems involving agriculture, natural resources, and state and local government.

On the San Francisco campus, since 1874, there have been courses dealing with the increasingly complex legal responsibilities of the physician to society. The Regents granted legal medicine departmental status in 1958.

The University has also initiated organized research units, largely supported by foundation grants, which inquire into the present interactions between increasingly complex laws and a rapidly changing community. At Berkeley, the Center for the Study of Law and Society, founded in 1961, studies such questions as the social foundations of due process in industry, the evolution of controls within professional associations, and the problems of governing large universities. A large share of its attention is directed to critical examination of the whole process of the

Practice Court, School of Law, UCLA

administration of criminal justice and of the process and effects of juvenile court laws. At UCLA, the Law-Science Research Center, founded 1963, conducts research into the impact of science on the rule of law in society, especially the impact of the computer and its capacities for the processing, storage, and retrieval of legal data on decision-making, not only by courts of law, but by the legislatures and eventually by all branches of government.

The purpose of these mock trials is to approximate as closely as possible the actual conduct of litigation. The judge presides with the full authority of experience, contributing to the training of young lawyers from love of the profession. The members of the local bar, who, without compensation, act as advisory council to the teams of student attorneys, advising them on the preparation of their briefs and at the counsel table during trial, will join with the judge and the school's permanent faculty on grading each "firm" for professional conduct, cooperation, and industry. Each firm is limited to three witnesses; plaintiff and defendant are occasionally sought through the theater arts department, and technical witnesses through the professional schools. The jury is drawn from the UCLA student body or from local high school senior government classes. Court is called promptly at 4:00 P.M. every Thursday, and runs strictly on schedule. All cases must be concluded by 10:00 P.M.

College of Environmental Design, Berkeley

The college, composed of four departments—architecture, city and regional planning, design, and landscape architecture—reflects the effort of the University to achieve a synthesis of the disciplines responsible for the man-made environment of California. Architecture began at the University when the great Bernard Maybeck, coming in 1894 to teach engineering students instrumental drawing and descriptive geometry, discovered in his class a half dozen undergraduates so interested in the design of buildings that he invited them to his home for an informal course in architecture. Formally, the department began in 1903 under John Galen Howard, supervising architect for the campus development plan, to whom Berkeley owes its central classic axis and landmarks such as the Campanile and Greek Theatre. Landscape architecture began in 1913 within the College of Agriculture as the Division of Landscape Gardening and Horticulture, and design in 1919 as the Department of Household Art in the College of Letters and Science. After World War II,

recognition of the rapid changes taking place in our urban civilization resulted in an independent Department of City and Regional Planning in 1948.

In 1950, William Wilson Wurster, a Berkeley alumnus noted for his contributions to architecture in the San Francisco Bay Area, returned from the East, where he had been dean of the School of Architecture and Planning at Massachusetts Institute of Technology, to become dean of architecture at Berkeley. He was among the first to perceive the need for interdisciplinary research, planning, and professional education to deal with the total environment of man, and assumed leadership in the formation of the College of Environmental Design in 1959. The striking concrete building named in honor of Wurster, now dean emeritus, and his late wife Catherine, is the most passionately debated structure on the Berkeley campus. It houses an extensive library, design studios, and seminar rooms for all of the college's departments, as well as special-purpose workshops equipped with kilns for ceramics, looms for textiles, and shops for making architectural models.

For twelve hundred students, undergraduate and graduate, this building is the headquarters from which they disperse to attend classes and seminars that reach into the vast resources of the Berkeley campus. The Institute of Urban and Regional Development and its subsidiaries, the Center for Planning and Development Research and the Center for Real Estate and Urban Economics conduct studies and make forecasts of urban and regional problems in California, the nation, and the world.

Urban Renewal Project, College of Environmental Design, Berkeley

Graduate students propose solutions for the many problems vexing the Mission District in San Francisco.

School of Architecture and Urban Planning, UCLA

Opening in the fall of 1966, the school launched its initial program at a graduate level: an intensive two-year course designed to bridge the distance between the architect concerned with individual structures and the urban planner dealing with the physical, economic, legal, and sociological dynamics of the region. Candidates for the Master of Architecture in Urban Design degree had already to possess the Bachelor of Architecture degree and a college level knowledge of economics, sociology, and political science; of the applicants, only those whose exhibits of work accomplished showed exceptional design ability were accepted. The dean of the new school, George A. Dudley, A.I.A., who had served as secretary to the U. N. Advisory Planning Board and as director of the New York State Office for Regional Development, chose as associates brilliant planners from widely different origins: Henry C. K. Liu, born in Hong Kong and educated in the United States; Peter Kamnitzer, born in Germany, graduate education in the United States, and once assistant to the National Planning Board of the Government of Israel; Denise V. Scott Brown, born in South Africa and trained in England; and, as lecturer, Calvin Hamilton, planning director formerly of the city of Pittsburgh and currently of the city of Los Angeles. The course they scheduled—right down to "interdisciplinary lunches"—aimed first at defining urban form, forces, and functions, and the superb technologies of engineering and economics, already developed, but often, from lack of planning, misapplied. UCLA faculty from disciplines as diverse as urban sociology, land economics, transportation, law, public health, business administration, air pollution, and psychology came to give their often sharply conflicting view of the same situation: the school believes there are seldom clear alternatives, and the urban designer must resolve the conflicts, achieve order from confusion, and give an abstract conclusion a beautiful, humanly satisfying form. The panel of visitors who come to give anything from a single lecture to a ten-week course includes such figures as Serge Chermayeff, Buckminster Fuller, and I. M. Pei; local visitors include Charles Eames, Victor Gruen, Richard Neutra, and William Pereira. Before a

School of Architecture and Urban Planning, UCLA

Dean George A. Dudley and Henry C. K. Liu discuss student design for a scientific laboratory complex in a mountain area. Mr. Liu comments on the school: "Los Angeles is growing so fast that there is very little difference between it and an entirely new city. Most of the problems of this city with which we will be dealing at the School of Architecture and Urban Planning have world-wide implications. When we talk about new towns, we're not just talking about them in California, but in Africa, Asia and Australia; possibly new settlements in outer space. Nevertheless, the problems in Los Angeles are so far ahead of those elsewhere in the world that when we talk about the future we're talking about the advance trends of the present in this city. In that sense, Los Angeles is a kind of laboratory for our work."

jury drawn from professionals, as well as the faculty, technical experts, and knowledgeable laymen, the student must present his work in both its intermediate and final forms, and debate in public the validity of his decisions.

As it grows, through further graduate, undergraduate, and professional programs dealing with practical problems on all levels and helping new theoretical concepts to evolve, the school hopes to become "a truly experimental laboratory for the betterment of our environment."

Engineering

In addition to its many engineering departments on most campuses, the University maintains, on the industrial flats beside the San Francisco Bay at Richmond, a number of engineering laboratories, some financed almost entirely by grants from industry and the state of California, and others operated for the United States government. Here the many problems presented by an increasingly congested population are explored. Traffic safety devices are tested here; new methods of seawater conversion are investigated; ways to purify air and water are sought; improved systems to eliminate the causes of pollution are invented. Ship models are subjected to simulated wave and current conditions in a towing tank; the shoaling of estuarial sediments is studied. Many experiments with algae are being conducted to determine their possible use as food, or as a purifying agent, or as a source of air and water during long space flights.

Airport Runway Lighting Laboratory, Richmond Field Station

The fact that every nation tends to have its own runway lighting system has become a matter of international concern: in these days of jet flight, the same pilot may within a few hours be landing at airports halfway round the world, each of which may have a different pattern of airport runway and approach lighting. In the stress of landing, expecially at night under conditions of poor visibility, the difficulty of remembering what an unfamiliar pattern signifies might cause crashes and collisions. At the request of the United States Federal Aviation Agency, the University's Institute of Transportation and Traffic Engineering has built a fog chamber where all conditions of visibility down close to zero-zero can be produced and maintained for any desired period.

Three major lighting systems, those of the United States, the United Kingdom, and the Dutch, were installed on a one-tenth scale. The little plane cockpit starts its descent at 25 feet (250 feet to scale) and flies at 15 miles per hour (150 miles per hour to scale). Pilots in various stages of stress and fatigue are brought in to "fly" the cockpit and to experience each of the systems under varying visibilities. Most pilots, on their first ride, as they approach the simulated 100-foot level, when the decision whether to land or abort must be made, instinctively reach for controls which aren't there. The University plans to simulate such controls, as well as other conditions of flight, so more realistic test conditions will prevail. The University recommends a blend of the United States and Dutch lighting systems which has already been provisionally approved by the International Civil Aircraft Organization. Next the laboratory will tackle the problems of how to dissipate fog, rain, and drizzle from airport approaches.

Structural Research Laboratory, Richmond Field Station

This huge Universal Testing Machine, with four million pounds maximum pressure, and sixty-five feet in overall height, is famous in engineering history. It tested the stanchions for the Golden Gate Bridge, worked eighteen hours a day during World War II on solving naval problems, and now examines for strength and tension, compression and cross-bending, various components of jet planes and space craft. Other machines nearby simulate wave action greater than any hurricane or typhoon, or initiate earth-quake tremors, to the possible limits of the Richter scale, or subject girders and timbers to increasing load, while gauges record the stresses and strains. Some types of tests continue for years, as the engineers working on industrial products or on immense and complicated federal projects return again and again with improved materials and structures to subject them to the rigors of this testing laboratory.

In the adjacent Fire Laboratory, walls are built and slid into furnaces where flames from batteries of gas jets attack them for specified numbers of hours. The fire-resistance of shakes and shingles is tested by the equivalent of a burning brand thrown upon them at the lip of a wind tunnel wherein a gale is generated.

John T. Middleton, professor of plant pathology at Riverside

Former director of the University's Statewide Air Pollution Research Center, Middleton is now on leave serving as director of the new National Center for Air Pollution Control, a branch of the United States Department of Health, Education and Welfare, Washington, D.C.

Statewide Air Pollution Research Center, Riverside

John T. Middleton, former director of the Statewide Air Pollution Research Center and professor of plant pathology at Riverside, was the first to discover that smog was damaging crops in southern California. Following this discovery in 1944, a research program was developed at Riverside. In the laboratories and greenhouses, Middleton and his associates analyzed the components of smog, and tested the effects of each, alone or in combination, at varying densities during night and day. But as smog increased, so did the scope of its damage. Middleton warned that the air has become "a malfunctioning sewer....The time has come for us to conserve our air resources as we do water, forests and game."

Smog now threatens every urbanized and industrialized area in the world. In mild attacks, it may merely irritate eyes and lungs; in serious attacks, it can kill.

The sources of pollution are many and complex—motor vehicles, jet planes, industry, power plants, domestic heating, and agricultural burning. Atmospheric inversion trapping fumes from these sources between mountain barriers or within other natural "airshed" basins intensifies the problem. The automobile, of course, is a chief offender; the effects of auto smog controls are being offset by increasing numbers of cars and continually denser traffic. Controls much more strict and effective must be devised, and new, non-polluting sources of energy must be developed to replace the fossil fuels. Economically feasible ways for industries to reclaim waste fumes and gases must be found. If the cost of pollution control appears enormous, it must be seen in perspective against the incalculable costs of uncontrolled pollution—soiling and damaging of buildings, agricultural crop loss, rotting of fabrics, and damage to man's health. New social, economic, and governmental tools are needed to cope with what is already a regional menace, seeping down coasts, creeping through mountain passes. The wind does not stop at city or state or national boundaries.

To bring to bear on these appallingly complex problems the full force of the University's faculty and research resources, the Statewide Air Pollution Research Center was established in 1961 at Riverside. The center serves as a central agency to stimulate. solicit, support, and coordinate research in critical areas; sponsor and encourage graduate and post-doctoral participation; and present timely information through all media of communication. Many of the statewide staff serve as advisors to institutions and industries, as well as city, county, state, federal, and international organizations. Air pollution is an evil and unexpected consequence of an urban and mechanized society, and only society itself can control and eliminate it.

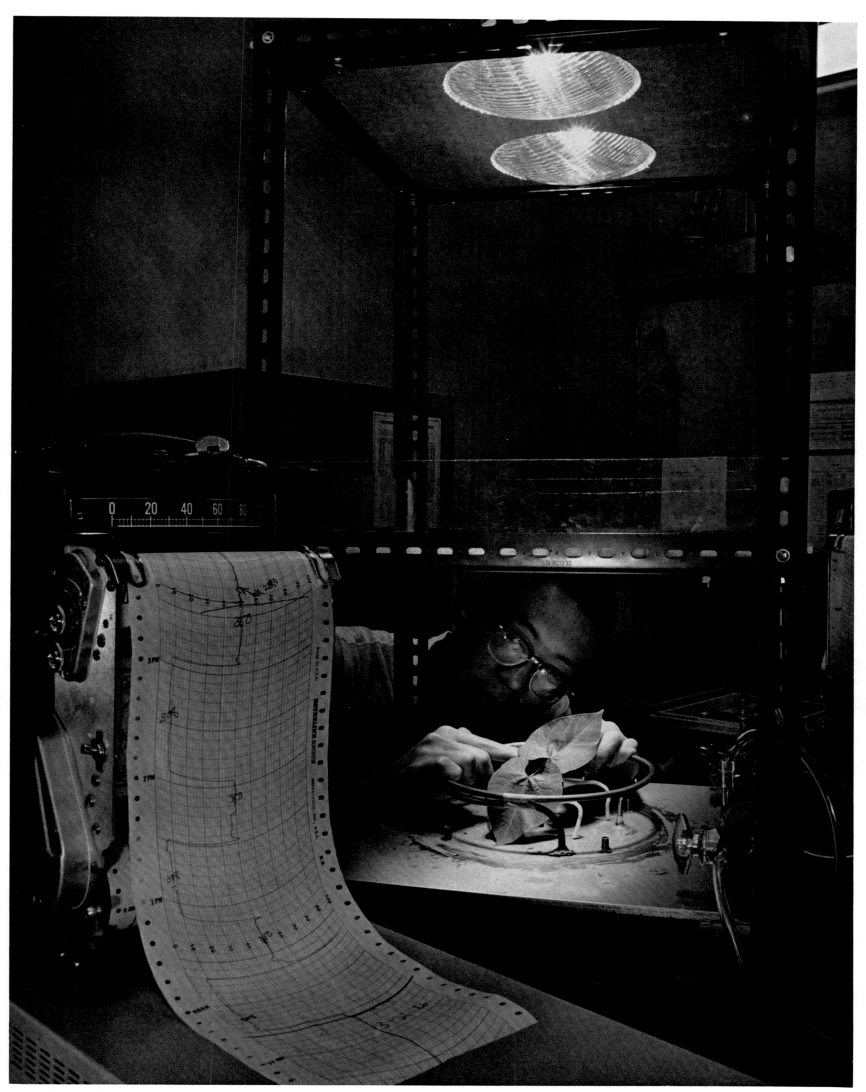

Statewide Air Pollution Research Center, Riverside

Measuring the effect of cement dust on photosynthesis.

University Extension

In half an hour this quiet campus will blaze with light. Crowds will be coming from the surrounding megalopolis to attend classes, concerts, plays, films, poetry readings, exhibitions, dance programs, and other events. Much of this activity will be due to University Extension. All over the state, there will be other meetings, lectures, conferences, and seminars; for University Extension, in addition to bringing the people to the campus, has always gone to them.

In 1893 when it began, University Extension was literally extension. Professors traveled from the Berkeley campus to give adults, at night, courses similar to those they gave undergraduates by day. And the public was invited to the campus to share in special events, such as a concert or lecture by a distinguished visitor. These services were soon perceived to be inadequate: the adult community had more complex needs and desires. University Extension became more mobile and responsive. What, as individuals, did adults *need* to know in order to conduct their lives, homes, jobs, or professions with satisfaction to themselves? What did they *yearn* to know for their personal enrichment, curiosity, and delight? What about the background necessary to understand world events? What of some basic intro-duction to the revolutions taking place in the arts and sciences? Next, as citizens, what should people know? What, in the largest sense, were the most pressing public needs and problems?

University Extension, listening and analyzing, projecting and organizing the most effective methods of presentation for each idea and issue, became not only the largest, but the most imaginative and dynamic, extension service in the United States. Under its own dean, Paul Sheats (based in Los Angeles), who, like the chancellors, is directly responsible to the President, it is known as the "tenth campus." Yet it receives very little state support, depending chiefly upon fees and on grants and contracts from foundations, corporations, and government agencies.

Moonrise, UCLA

Poster, San Francisco Extension Center

Around a quarter of a million people a year attend University Extension programs—about one in every twenty who attend continuing education programs in the United States.

From the professions, enrollment includes one of every two doctors and lawyers in the state, one of every five dentists, one of every eight engineers, and one of every twelve teachers. Architects and landscape architects enroll, as do social workers, law enforcement officers, union officials, and business executives, including company presidents and chairmen of the board. Members of nearly every profession attend short courses, symposia, conferences, and summer institutes for postgraduate, professional credit. The "knowledge explosion" is so dynamic that what a man learns today may be obsolete in five years, and what he will need to know in ten years has not yet been discovered. Continuing Education of the Bar, Continuing Education in Medicine and the Health Sciences, Continuing Education in Environmental Design, Continuing Education in Criminology, Engineering, Real Estate, and Social Welfare—these are some of University Extension's programs which annually assemble, assess, and present vital new discoveries and techniques. In many cases the information offered has not yet been published, and the course or conference may result in another of the University Extension's hundreds of handbooks, workbooks, and textbooks.

For personal enrichment, thousands of people from all professions, vocations and degrees of eminence enroll. Nobel Laureate Willard Libby, professor of chemistry at UCLA, after lecturing in the extension series, "Peacetime Uses of Space," enrolled in another University Extension course; so did violinist Jascha Heifetz, after conducting a master course for accomplished musicians.

University Extension offers more than six thousand courses a year. They include programs enabling doctors to confer with colleagues in Japan, Hong Kong, Mexico, and Israel; residential programs studying the arts in Europe; seminars on a region in terms of its ethnic, cultural, and economic problems, which culminate in an expeditionary visit; multi-nation, graduate-level courses preparing Peace Corps volunteers and Agency for International Development personnel for service overseas; a conference on "Law Enforcement and Racial and Cultural Tensions" held in Berkeley, which assembled the most outstanding experts in the field; a "World Conference on Pre-stressed Concrete," which drew more than a thousand educators, scientists, and engineers from thirty-two countries, including the Union of Soviet Socialist Republics; a "Summer Institute in Regional Science," where businessmen came to study the problems of metropolitan and regional areas and analytical methods for their solution; and a five day conference on the "Creative Person" held at Lake Tahoe, where the findings of the University on creativity were presented to an audience composed of the heads of foundations and research institutes, presidents of corporations, and a representative from the White House. University Extension courses are offered at more than two hundred and fifty locations in the state annually. Special courses, workshops, and seminars are held in studios, union halls, factories, and even private living rooms. Extension courses are offered at every University campus, of course, and at University Extension centers in San Francisco and Los Angeles. Courses or workshops that last for weekends or several days at a time are often held at the Alumni Center near Lake Tahoe, at Asilomar, and at the Residential Conference Center at Lake Arrowhead. Students can take courses in their own homes, by correspondence or television.

Continuing Education in Business Administration, Los Angeles

Neil H. Jacoby, professor of business administration and dean of the School of Business Administration at Los Angeles, addresses a group of executives who meet one afternoon a week for a full academic year.

Residential Conference Center, Lake Arrowhead

Distractions, responsibilities, smog, traffic, and crowds have been left behind, down below the huge rampart called the Rim of the World. Up among the mile-high peaks of the San Bernardino Mountains, its lodge and cottages set among pines and junipers near the lake, the conference center is a place to relax and to concentrate. The 120 people—the maximum the center can accommodate—have all been drawn to this conference by an intense interest in the subject presented. Living and learning are informal. Lectures are given in the living rooms. Discussion groups meet in the patios or out under the trees, by the pool or the brook. If the conference has scheduled an hour or so free in the afternoons, one can nap, swim, hike, or go in for any sport the season suggests. If not, there are lectures and discussions, beginning and ending officially as the conference is scheduled, but informally continuing as long as one pleases.

The center's schedule is jammed the year around. Usually there is only an hour and a half between the departure of one group and the arrival of the next, with its wholly different character, desires, hours, and even menus. A workshop in computer design which hardly pauses long enough to eat is followed by a liberal arts conference which enjoys leisure in the afternoons. Next comes a group of doctors interested in the latest discoveries in gastro-intestinal circulation; they, apparently, never stop talking even to sleep. On their heels comes a 4-H Club workshop, the Academic Senate, or a conference on community problems. Usually each group comes for three days, which is all most people can spare. But, in the opinion of the professional University Extension staff, it is the longer conferences of perhaps five days that offer their participants the most refreshing and illuminating learning experience.

Labor Day Conference on the "Mastery of Life": Dr. Jonas Salk, developer of the polio vaccine, leads a discussion group.

Residential Conference Center, Lake Arrowhead

University Extension Director Carl Tjerandsen and Stevenson College Residence Houses, Santa Cruz

On every campus, especially the new and developing ones, University Extension service is a bridge between the University and the community. What is the inherent character of the community? What kind of programs are likely to interest and stimulate it? Does it have large segments of people with special educational needs, or a reservoir of skills and talents that could fountain up into a center dazzling and unique, like the Theatre Group at UCLA, which University Extension evoked from the theatrical community of Los Angeles? And what are the community's problems concerning such matters as air pollution, traffic, water shortages, housing, schools, and racial tensions? The University has many years experience in such fields and special knowledge accumulated through research and surveys by thousands of dedicated faculty and graduate students. University Extension would like to do for the urban community what Agricultural Extension has done for the rural community: make the resources of the University available to all citizens who need them. University Extension envisages classes, lectures, and discussion groups in every city and town, with people coming out of them motivated by new knowledge and new goals.

University Extension Concert, Royce Hall, UCLA

Composer Calvin Jackson conducting a rehearsal of his "Skyscraper." Clarence Jackson, Ulysses Kay, and William Grant Sill also conducted their own works as part of the survey program, "The Negro and the Arts."

University Extension at Home, Beverly Hills

A course in "The Art of Seeing Art" meets one night a week for ten weeks not only in the living rooms of course members but also in museums and galleries.

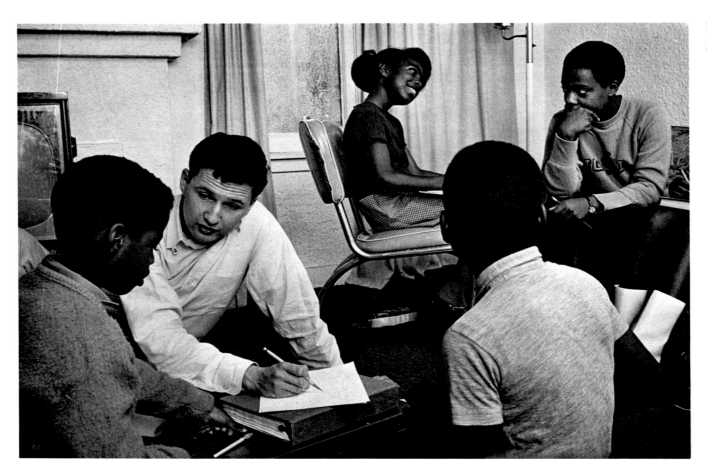

Student Volunteers in Community Service

As a national movement, and one distinct from earlier and more traditional forms of community service, the student tutorial programs stem from the southern civil rights movement of the early 1960's, when undergraduates, many for the first time, came face to face with the desperate plight of the very poor, especially among racial minority groups. Illiterate, bewildered, deprived, and defenseless, these people needed constant, personal help in their day-to-day struggles against enormous handicaps. Again and again, students were told by people of their own age and even younger, "It's too late for me. Start with the kids." Demonstrations began to look like super-ficial gestures, useful now and then, perhaps, but the real human need was here, basic, beyond politics.

Back on campus, students sought ways to help in the Negro ghettos, the Mexican migrant worker camps, the Indian reservations. Often they had to find their own contacts and pay the costs of their projects out of their own lean pockets. Then, as the projects proved their value and students of all kinds of backgrounds and political beliefs began volunteering by the hundreds, support came in from the associated students' unions, from school systems, and from community and federal agencies such as the Office of

Economic Opportunity. At Berkeley, the volunteers could work through the University YWCA and Stiles Hall, the student YMCA. Stiles sponsors many programs, such as SWOP, Student West Oakland Project, which is designed to raise the academic level of minority group children in the schools. In 1965, SWOP had eighty volunteers; in 1966, six hundred. Through Stiles, a dozen upperclassmen and graduate students, often working toward degrees in law, criminology, psychology, and public health, go two or three times a week to San Quentin Prison, where they teach classes ranging from the functionally illiterate to potential college students. From Stiles, too, bilingual students go to Yuba City in the great heat of summer, to tutor Mexican children who have had to drop out of school again and again to follow their parents as they picked and canned fruit crops here and there throughout the state. Another group goes to Union City every week the year around, tutoring whole families; often the father and the children have only a smattering of English and the mother none at all.

At Riverside, in two years, student volunteers working as tutors and as assistants to teachers in the class-rooms built such warm and strong relationships between minority group parents and the teachers that they effected the complete integration of all the schools in the district. At Riverside too, some thirty volunteers run a "hangout" on one of the streets where Negroes and Mexicans feel free to stand and talk. The hangout has three parts: the office, where there is accurate and current information available on welfare, medical aid, legal counsel, employment, housing, voting, and education; the "living room," open to the whole community, where there are always coffee and magazines, and occasionally lectures and movies, and courses in Negro and Mexican history; and the "game room," with ping-pong, checkers, chess, and a record player for teen-agers who never had a place to go before. At UCLA, the Tutorial Project, backed by the Associated Students Union, did such magnificent work along the slum canals of Venice that the teachers of Los Angeles gave them an award for "Service to Youth in Education." At San Francisco, medical students, under faculty inspiration and supervision, go forth in Mobile Clinics to areas where no doctor or dentist has ever practiced; people who come may never have had a medical examination.

Every campus sponsors a summer camp for underprivileged children, and students raise funds through such events as, at Berkeley, for Cal Camp, the Ugly Man Contest and the Big C Sirkus, and, at UCLA, for Uni-Camp, the Mardi Gras festival. Students serve as counselors, frequently on a twenty-four-hour-a-day basis, for excited children out of the urban slums for the first time. At Uni-Camp there is a special ten-day session for blind children and another for diabetics.

In 1966, there were at the University of California more than eight thousand student volunteers, working at problems as various as their own gifts, backgrounds, and future careers. They work with the mentally retarded, the emotionally disturbed, the drop-outs and delinquents, as well as with school children and their parents and teachers. To tap hidden potentials, they organize art, music, and drama groups; to enliven community life, they also organize sports, dances, and picnics. Foreign students help too, lecturing on their native lands and displaying their costumes and dances. Many students take their vacations for work and study in other countries, showing little communities in Mexico how to build a school or a hospital, for example. The University of California has sent more graduates into the Peace Corps than any other university.

Most exciting of all to the volunteers is the University's own new goal of reflecting in its racial representation the total society. Urged by Clark Kerr, the Regents have made possible "a talent hunt" wherein students and graduate students, counseling various groups, watch for the brilliant but disadvantaged young—a Negro girl with an I.Q. of 140, who writes plays for her own delight and is a natural director, a Negro boy from Richmond who has an astonishing gift at moviemaking and the warmth to go back to Richmond and urge the other kids to work for college, a Chinese girl who is trilingual and makes and plays ancient musical instruments. Not to find such people would be society's loss. The University not only seeks them, but helps them enter the University and stay there.

Riverside student, senior in anthropology, with her tutee, a Navaho, at the Sherman Indian Institute

Berkeley student with her Mexican tutee in Golden Gate Park

Epilogue

On March 23, 1968, the University of California will enter its second century. Through eras of turbulence and eras of serene growth, it has gone on bringing the light of knowledge to all the concerns of mankind and the mysteries of the universe, for the benefit of its state and its people, the nation and the world.

Now it faces still greater challenges. As the focal point of knowledge in the most populous state in this nation, it is already applying its powers toward solving the manifold problems which now confront California and may soon confront the entire world in the new civilization fast shaping the future.

At a convocation in Berkeley in 1967, Chief Justice Earl Warren summarized the importance of the University to its state: "The University from its beginning planted its seed in every aspect of life in California, and today its roots are deep and pervasive in the economic, political and social structure of the state.... The state needs this University functioning at its highest potential, as it has been doing for nearly a hundred years....

"Californians, this is the time for us to do our utmost for the University because it has done its utmost for us. It is a time to encourage our distinguished faculty to pursue truth and knowledge into the darkest corners. It is a time to encourage them to teach the truth as they discover it. It is a time to give all the young people of our state the very best education we can afford."

To those who question the importance and the cost of supporting such education, the President's Commission on Higher Education answers: "It is an investment in free men. It is an investment in social welfare, better living standards, better health and less crime. It is an investment in a bulwark against garbled information, half-truths and untruths; against ignorance and intolerance. It is an investment in human talent, better human relationships, democracy, and peace."

The Sather Tower, Berkeley

Notes on the Photography

Throughout the project, natural light was used in every possible situation. Many exteriors demanded filters such as the Wratten #12 (minus Blue), the 23A (Orange-Red), and, occasionally, the #38 or #47 (Bluish) to increase the effect of atmospheric haze. The polarizer was used when lower sky values (and a slight reduction of haze effect) were desired—but without darkening of near shadow values.

The world exists in the light with which we see it; the intrusion of additional lighting may have questionable aesthetic effect. However, the limitations of the sensitive emulsions must be taken into account and it is quite proper to employ additional lighting to simulate the visual effect. The use of delicate fill-in illumination (such as reflected from a white umbrella or screen) will support the visual qualities of shadow areas which might otherwise fall beyond the range of the negative when the high values are properly rendered. Much fill-in illumination was provided by directing flashlight into the white umbrella; this gives a smooth distribution of soft light without obvious high-lights or shadow edges. For this, the Guide Number of the flash is about two-thirds that for an equivalent distance for direct flash. However, as the fill-in light is about one-half or one-fourth the full exposure for the subject under flash illumination alone, calculations must first consider the direct-light Guide Number for the particular shadow value desired. When working with daylight, the shadows have some illumination to begin with; the flash merely augments the shadow values.

Indoors, the problems are somewhat different. Many laboratories, etc. are illuminated by diffused fluorescent light, broad and shadowless, and this results in flat and somewhat textureless qualities, especially in the high-value areas. The addition of some directional light is helpful in such situations. There is always the temptation to contrive lighting situations and effects, and the results may be more dramatic than authentic. First, we begin with the existing light, and then apply additional light with restraint; we should work towards an effect which would be logical to the subject and to the area. Whenever possible, reflected light was used; direct flash or tungsten light was occasionally used, and "flash-in-the-pan" (flashlight at the camera) was used only occasionally with the small camera, under contrasty daylight conditions.

The many adjustments of the Sinar camera (view-camera type) were invaluable with architectural subjects, or with general subjects where great depth-of-field was required. The greater part of the work was done with the Hasselblad 500C camera, and quite a few pictures were made with the Zeiss Ikon Contarex camera. Type 55 P/N 4x5 Polaroid Land film was used with the 4x5 back on the Sinar camera.

In the majority of the pictures, contrast control was achieved by appropriate exposure and development of the negative (following my Zone System techniques). Many of the reproduction prints for this book were made on Du Pont Varigam with the Ferrante Codelight source instead of the conventional variable-contrast filters. Other prints were made on Kodabromide and Brovira. The prints for reproduction were scaled for the gravure printing process.

Finally, the general approach was intentionally forthright; the character of the subject did not favor highly stylized or forced images. The complex character of the University, its environment and its people, demanded a certain emphasis on reality. Also, the need for a unified book design and image quality required consistency throughout.

Appreciation is due many individuals and firms who gave most helpful advice on the many problems involved in this project.

A. A.

PRINCIPAL TECHNICAL DATA

CAMERAS 5x7 *Sinar,* with 4x5 reducing back.
5x7 sheet-film holders and 4x5 filmpack adapters (the 4x5 filmpack adapters were marked Normal, Normal-Plus, Normal-Minus, and Special. This simplified development procedures).
4x5 Polaroid film pack adapter.
Lenses: 12″ Voigtlander Apo-Collinear; 9¼″ Goerz Artar; 8″ Kodak Ektar; 121mm and 90mm Schneider Super-Angulons.
Hasselblad 500 C, with 50mm, 80mm, 120mm, 150mm, 250mm, and 500mm lenses (and appropriate accessories). Five 12-exp. magazines were used for various films and development methods.
Hasselblad Super-Wide, with 38mm lens.
Zeiss Ikon Contarex, with 21mm, 35mm, 85mm, and 135mm lenses, appropriate accessories.

LIGHTING EQUIPMENT Graflex Stroboflash (2 units)
Mecablitz 163
Colortran quartz-lamp system (2 units)
White reflecting umbrella

EXPOSURE METERS S.E.I. Exposure photometer
Weston Ranger IX Exposure Meter (with Ansel Adams' Zone System Dial)

ACCESSORIES Levels; small industrial Mirror (for setting lenses in crowded situations); Polarizers; Filters (3-inch gel for the larger lenses, and optical flats for the Hasselblad and Contarex cameras)

NEGATIVE MATERIAL Kodak Tri-X in 5x7 sheet film
4x5 film pack
120 and 35mm rolls
Kodak Pan-X in 5x7 sheet film
120 and 35mm rolls
Kodak Plus-X in 4x5 filmpacks
120 and 35mm rolls
Polaroid Land Type 55 P/N film packets (4x5)

NEGATIVE DEVELOPER Edwal FG 7 in various dilutions with water (sometimes with 9% sodium sulfite) and in conjunction with the alternate-waterbath process.

Colophon

This book has been designed by Nancy Newhall and Adrian Wilson.

The type is the University of California Old Style designed by Frederic W. Goudy especially for the University and set by the University of California Printing Department.

The printing has been executed by the Cardinal Company, San Francisco, under the supervision of Charles R. Wood.

Two processes are employed: photogravure for the plates, with varnish blocks, and photolithography for the type.

The paper is Warren's Lustro Dull and the binding cloth is Columbia Mills' Bradford Linen.